Upgrading Your Small Sailboat for Cruising

Upgrading Your Small Sailboat for Cruising

Paul and Marya Butler

International Marine Publishing Company
Camden, Maine

Published by International Marine Publishing Co., a division of Highmark Publishing Ltd., P.O. Box 220, Rt. 1, Camden, Maine 04843.

Typeset by Maryland Composition Co., Inc., Glen Burnie, MD
Printed and bound by BookCrafters, Chelsea, MI
Production by Janet Robbins
Line illustrations by Marya Butler
Cover design by Rod McCormick

10 9 8 7 6 5 4 3 2 1

Library of Congress Cataloging-in-Publication Data

Butler, Paul.
    Upgrading your small sailboat for cruising / Paul and Marya Butler.
        p.   cm.
    Includes index.
    ISBN 0-87742-960-X : $19.95
    1. Sailboats. 2. Boats and boating—Maintenance and repair.
I. Butler, Marya. II. Title.
VM351.B88 1988
623.8'223—dc19   88-12935
                                          CIP

For a tiny cabin and the mountains, lakes, and streams of Montana—the first place that has felt like home.

Contents

Acknowledgments

Much of the material presented here made its first appearance in various boating publications over the last few years, chiefly *Cruising World* and *Small Boat Journal*. We are grateful to the editors of those magazines for their assistance—in particular to Jim Brown, Dennis Caprio, Dan Segal, Tom Baker, and Richard Lebovitz of *Small Boat Journal*.

Most of all we are indebted to Cynthia Bourgeault of International Marine Publishing Company, who once again has helped to organize, clarify, and bring so many important details to our attention. May she always make the ferry on time.

Part I
Working with the Materials

Getting Started

This book has been written to stimulate confidence and creativity in undertaking improvement projects on your boat. While many of the projects described here are appropriate for any size boat, most are intended specifically for "small" sailboats, which to most people means less than 30 feet overall—a size range that takes maximum advantage of the simplicity and delight of boating.

Why modify small boats in the first place? For starters: safety, comfort, peace of mind, pride, and possibly resale value. The first two are by far the most important.

Safety means that your boat has sufficient ability to cope with whatever conditions you might encounter, whether gunkholing in the local millpond or on a world cruise. It means the rig has sufficient power to beat to windward without capsizing or swamping in head seas, and that the hull is tight and stout enough to handle rough water without breaking apart or leaking. Safety means that the boat will protect its passengers from the extremes of weather and exposure. Given the ever-changing vagaries of wind and water and such additional factors as length of fetch and extremes of temperature where you sail, there are usually many sensible improvements that can be made to any boat.

Production boats, though they may be priced right, are often built with more emphasis on surviving the rigors of business competition than the challenges of blue water and high winds. But production boats are also a great place to start, and with careful upgrading can become truly custom creations well suited to their owners' needs. With the help of modern materials and techniques, there is hardly a problem that can't be corrected to make a production boat better and stronger than new. Whether the problems were there from the start,

due to insufficient scantlings and inadequate construction techniques, or whether they have accumulated through hard use, there are multiple methods and materials to correct virtually any deficiency.

A neighbor of ours bought a much-used and obviously neglected Cal 20 sloop. It was a sound design, though built to light coastal scantlings and probably never intended for the kind of ambitious offshore cruising our friend had in mind. Because the boat was a bit worn, he got it for considerably less than the going price, and the money he saved he put into specific structural reinforcements. The entire deck-stepped mast support system was rebuilt. The deck was stiffened with external beams, and the hull was reinforced with interior frames laminated onto the hull in vulnerable areas. With some other small repairs and patching, some cabinetry, and a coat of new paint, he ended up with a boat that was stronger and better looking than when it had come off the production line. As a result of the improvements he also knew the boat intimately and was thus much better prepared to cope with any problems that might occur in the future. The projects were accomplished without prior boatbuilding experience—when he started he was a person who for years had considered himself "all thumbs" and in fact hardly knew which end of a hammer to hold.

While the emphasis in this book is on single-skin fiberglass hulls, many of the projects and techniques will work equally well on foam-sandwich or balsa-core fiberglass hulls, plank-on-frame wood, cold-molded wood, aluminum, and steel. Many are equally applicable to powerboats. The ideas presented here are intended primarily as upgrading projects for existing boats, but they may also be useful to builders planning original construction. Built to sufficient scantlings the first time around, a boat might never require additional reinforcements, and such forethought contributes to safety and resale value, not to mention to builders' reputations. Many of these ideas were developed and refined as improvements on traditional design solutions when we were building boats for clients.

In addition to reinforcing existing structures, upgrading small boats often involves adding entirely new structures. Many small production craft have a minimum of equipment, and even items one would be inclined to label "vital" must sometimes be added on. To cite just one example, we've seen foredeck hatches eliminated on many small cruisers that obviously need them for safety, convenience, and utility. These were left out in the interest of keeping the price as low as possible, but as a result, the safety- and comfort-minded boat-owner faces a time-consuming retrofit. Cutting the hole for the access hatch is only a small part of the job—the bare access hole requires framing, coamings, and, of course, a strong, watertight hatch cover.

The projects in this book run the gamut from the more decorative (like some of the canvas and netting ideas) to purely functional, nitty-gritty beef-ups in critical areas such as mast support, floor timbers, and chainplates. Each boat will have its weak points, its Achilles' heel, and according to the level of your personal experience, it might be best to complete one or two less demanding projects before attempting something like a major structural overhaul requiring considerable time and effort. As is usual with boats, much depends on specific circumstances of location, weather, and the design and hull material of the boat, not to mention your own personal variables such as attitude, confidence, and motivation. We provide as much general and specific information as seems applicable to help you assess the scope and complexity of each project.

A big part of each project—sometimes it seems like 99 percent of the entire job—is getting tools and materials on hand. Once everything is in place: the extension cords routed to the proper location, the fresh blades put in the saws, the chisels sharpened, the epoxy mixer and fillers on hand, and so on and so on, the actual job may take only a few minutes. The amateur weekend builder shouldn't be discouraged by this because the professional builder faces the same, if not more complex, logistics and learns to accept them as part of the job.

Readers will find considerable mention of epoxy throughout this book, and in fact, many of the projects included here would not be possible without it. Epoxy has simplified and routinized operations that were once considered highly complicated and possible only for experienced professionals. The fact that it adheres tenaciously to clean, cured polyester resin and fiberglass (the stuff of all fiberglass hulls) makes it remarkably well suited to modifying and strengthening glass hulls. (Indeed, to our way of thinking, the perfect fiberglass hull would use epoxy resin instead of fiberglass resin, but epoxy is more temperamental to mix and apply and more expensive than polyester, which by itself is enough to scuttle those thoughts among most production builders.)

There are various brands of epoxy available and a lot of hype in the marketplace. For the past 15 years we have used WEST system epoxy from the Gougeon Brothers of Bay City, Michigan, in a variety of situations and conditions, without a single problem and with the benefit of a lot of good advice and information from the supplier. The Gougeons also supply good instructional literature and safety information for those not accustomed to working with epoxy, which does take a bit of getting used to. Epoxy requires some simple but specialized techniques, and there are many additives and enhancing materials which, when used with epoxy, become ideal boatbuilding and boat-modifying devices. Specifics will be covered later in this book.

Safety is a big concern when using epoxy because it is significantly more toxic than polyesters. We work absolutely "clean," which means we never allow uncured epoxy to touch our skin. We also use vigorous ventilation when working below decks or in small areas, and we have developed building techniques that seldom if ever require us to sand epoxy, thus eliminating the problem of dealing with dust by not producing it in the first place. With boatbuilding projects in general, and with epoxy in particular, a workmanlike attitude emphasizing order and cleanliness can spell the difference between comfort and misery—and between success and failure.

The owner who does his or her own work can expect to make decent wages in the process from the money saved. Check out the hourly rate at your local boatyards and reward yourself accordingly when the job is complete!

Most important, don't be afraid to use your own creativity in further modifying or adapting these projects to your own specific circumstances. Few of the ideas here are really new; most are refinements of existing design solutions, developed by experimenting with the materials and taking an idea one step further. Feel free to do likewise.

Happy upgrading!

Basic Tools and Techniques

For the most part, the projects in this book draw on familiar carpentry skills: cutting, fitting, fastening, finishing. If you own a small glass production boat, the unfamiliar element may lie in how to transpose these traditional woodworking skills to the realm of fiberglass and epoxy. Healthy fiberglass is a tough material. With a strong, well-maintained gelcoat, it has excellent abrasion resistance and substantial puncture resistance—which you will quickly realize the first time you try to drill or cut into it. Fiberglass carpentry is not all that difficult, but it does take some getting used to, and some specialized tools and techniques.

Cutting and Drilling Fiberglass

Drills and Bits
Drilling accurate, clean holes into the laminate requires sharp drill bits, and it may be necessary to centerpunch lightly or score the gelcoat surface to get an accurate start. Metal- and wood-cutting drill bits both work, but sharp metal cutting bits may work slightly better for drilling through laminates ½ inch and thicker. Butterfly wood-cutting bits, also known as spade bits, don't usually work well on fiberglass laminate even when they are sharp, and we usually resort to conventional metal- or wood-cutting bits. Drilling through fiberglass tends to dull even good laminated steel bits in a short time, so prepare to sharpen periodically.

Scoring a line on the gelcoat as a guide for drilling or cutting is best accomplished by holding a straightedge or wood template

Tapered wood bits, countersinks, and stop collars, with allen wrenches for adjustment.

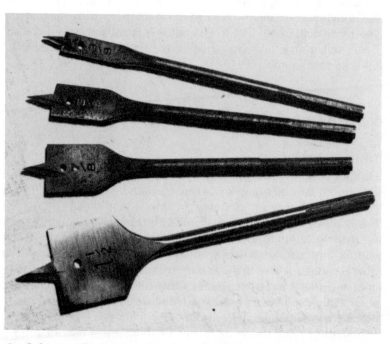

Spade bits usually do not work well on fiberglass, even when they are sharp.

Shaped carborundum stones, called "slips," are used for sharpening bits of all types.

This carbide-tipped Formica cutter is ideal for scoring gelcoat.

against the gelcoat surface and pulling a sharp tool along the edge. An ideal tool for marking or scoring gelcoat is a sharp carbide tooth on a handle, such as is normally used for scoring plastic laminates, but an awl or even a sharp nail will do the job. An ink marker is sometimes handy for drawing guide patterns on gelcoat or cured laminate, as long as the mark is removed by cutting away.

If you are making a cutout for an oval, round, or oddly shaped portlight or other piece of hardware, it may be easier to drill holes at corners, at intervals along the perimeter, or both, and then cut between the holes with a jigsaw, much like a "connect the dots" drawing. When cutting small-diameter holes for transducers and through-hull fittings, try to do as much of the cutting as possible with a small-diameter drill bit; then knock out the center plug and finish the job to precise fit with an oval or round rasp.

Saws

Professional-quality hole saws with mandrels are an alternative way of making clean, small-diameter holes (up to three or four inches) for through-hulls. But unless the hole saw has carbide teeth it will last for only a few cuts—maybe only one cut in thick glass—before it becomes uselessly dull and you find yourself burning slowly through the laminate instead of cutting a clean hole. If you do a lot of small hole cutting in glass hulls, carbide teeth are a wise investment. Not only do they last much longer than high-speed steel teeth, they also do a better job.

Jigsaws are the old standby for cutting fiberglass laminate, and a hand-held jigsaw with a scrolling head is a particular blessing because it allows you to cut arcs and circles while hanging upside down in the bilge, standing under the boat with the saw extended overhead, or working in tight corners. If you can afford to double up on your power tools, it's a smart idea to keep one jigsaw exclusively for fiberglass work, to avoid wear and tear on your good wood-cutting tools. The abrasive glass dust is hard on quality tools.

It helps to have a large assortment of extra blades on hand, from fine-tooth metal-cutting blades to rough- and fine-tooth wood-cutting blades, and including a few wider, flush-cutting blades for working up against coamings and decks. A blade usually will last for only a few feet of cutting in thick, cured fiberglass anyway; once it is dull it will either start to burn without cutting, or else it will break. Forcing the blade will only break it sooner, and overheats your saw motor as well. Stopping every few inches or so to let the blade cool will make

2" DIA.
HOLE SAW
WITH CARBIDE TEETH

it last longer, but few people seem to have the patience for this. (If you cut a lot of fiberglass with a jigsaw, you will probably learn where you can buy blades in bulk packaging.) If the blade bends sideways, stop and let it cool, then bend it back straight; otherwise you will be spending a lot of time with a rasp trying to clean up the sides of the cut.

Some types of jigsaws seem to have more success cutting glass than others, and it pays to experiment. Some have a slight rotary action instead of a straight-up-and-down blade movement, and many saws have adjustable power settings or blade speeds. This latter feature can be a real advantage, for slower speeds seem to preserve the blade slightly longer than fast speeds, and also make a cleaner cut. We have a heavy old Sears roller bearing jigsaw with blade speeds that graduate from 1 to 12; at a medium or slow speed with plenty of sharp blades it does a quite satisfactory job. By all rights it should have been retired with honors, but it continues to plug along, and I now use it exclusively for cutting fiberglass.

Panel saws and circular saws (Skilsaw is a popular brand) can be used for making relatively straight, fast cuts in flatter sections of fiberglass. Carbide blades are again a necessity if you expect to cut more than a few inches before the blade overheats and gets uselessly dull. Circular saws also generate considerable fiberglass dust, which not only ruins bearings in power tools but can pose a significant health threat (see ahead, under Sanding). Respirators for dust and goggles for eye protection are a necessity; ear protection is also advisable.

Routers

Routers with carbide bits make the cleanest possible cuts in fiberglass, and with a minimum of dust. Routers turn at very high speeds and require some experience to get the best out of them, but they are the tool of choice when cutting in relatively flat areas of the hull and deck—as, for example, when installing hatches. There is a variety of cutter bits available for ¼-inch-shaft routers (the standard home handyman model), and an even wider variety of specialized bits for larger professional routers with ½-inch-diameter shafts.

A router bit normally turns clockwise, and the cut has to be made against that clockwise rotation to prevent dangerous skipping. It becomes evident very soon if you are moving the bit in the wrong direction. An edge guide or template is required to control the bit; free-handing a router is not only dangerous, but usually results in sloppy work and possibly disaster. The only exception is when you have to remove a lot of material from a given area to a specific depth. In that case, it usually works well to crisscross the area with the router and use the resulting cuts as a depth guide for removing the balance of the material with a chisel or sander.

A typical ¼-inch-shaft router with a small carbide V-groove bit.

The cutting and trimming bits we most often use are ¼-inch-wide straightface bits with two carbide flutes (cutting edges). Depending on the project, we use them either with or without a sleeve. A sleeve is an attachment, available for various types of routers, that screws into the base of the router to act as a permanent edge guide for the bit. It allows somewhat more precise control than using the base of the router aligned against a batten or straightedge for the same purpose. The sleeve fits to within less than an inch of the cutting bit, whereas the base of the router is usually some three inches away from the cutting bit edge. Another type of carbide bit, not commonly seen but available from specialty tool shops, has a roller bearing on top of the cutter flutes. The edge of the bearing is aligned flush with the surface of the cutters. The advantage—and it is a substantial advantage—is that it allows a template (pattern) to be made to the exact size as the hole to be cut, which enables a visual inspection before cutting. You can also make plunge cuts (cuts started without a pilot hole) with this type of router bit.

Templates and Edge Guides. Long battens or wood straightedges can be screwed temporarily to the deck or hull of a glass boat to serve as an edge guide for the router; after the cutting is done, they are removed and the holes filled with dabs of epoxy. Duct tape will sometimes hold a guide batten in place securely enough to allow making the cut; if not, you can position a helper on either end of the batten to hold it in place. In some instances, where control seems difficult no matter what you do, it may be best to resort to a jigsaw, although the router is faster and neater.

Templates for standard size portholes, hatch cutouts, through-hull fittings, deck irons, and other such items can be made from solid-

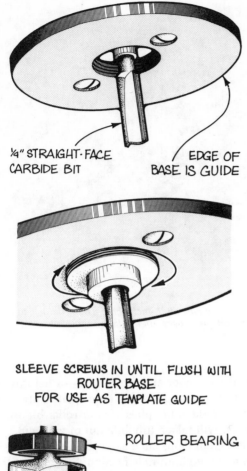

¼" STRAIGHT-FACE
CARBIDE BIT

EDGE OF
BASE IS GUIDE

SLEEVE SCREWS IN UNTIL FLUSH WITH
ROUTER BASE
FOR USE AS TEMPLATE GUIDE

ROLLER BEARING

¾" STRAIGHT-FACE
BIT CUTS FLUSH

SAVE FACTORY EDGE OF PLYWOOD FOR A STRAIGHTEDGE

4"- 6" WIDE PIECE CUT ON TABLE SAW
FOR PERFECT PARALLEL

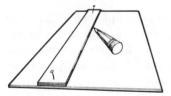

½" PLYWOOD (STIFF) GOOD
FOR FLAT SURFACES.....

THINNER PLY
LIKE ⅛" (FLEXIBLE)
BEST FOR CURVED SURFACES
LIKE CABIN SIDES

Four carbide-tipped router bits, all ¼-inch shaft size. From left to right: ½-inch bullnose or rounding bit, cove, ogee, and ⅜-inch rabbet bit.

core plywood and used over and over again—a helpful shortcut if you do a lot of retrofit work. But avoid poor-quality plywood, which tends to have voids in the inner plies; if your roller bit or sleeve falls into a small void, it will take a tiny bite out of your cut.

Templates for small items such as portholes or through-hull fittings are often made doughnut-hole fashion: first cut out the desired pattern on the plywood; then use the "doughnut" (the plywood with the hole in the middle) rather than the "hole" (the cutout piece itself) as your guide. Depending on whether you are using a sleeve or the edge of the router base as a cutting guide, the template must be made exactly that much larger than the hole to be cut. For best control, it may be necessary to make the final half inch of the cut with a section of hacksaw blade held in a pair of Vise-Grips.

Sanding and Finishing

Serious sanding of fiberglass is most easily accomplished with a large disc sander and a fresh, dry, aggressive grit pad with stiff backing. If you have to smooth the inside surface of a hull for laminating on more glass, or if there are drips and hairs left over from a sloppy laminating job when the hull was built, a two-speed disc sander with a relatively small-diameter, 6-inch disc is about as useful a tool as you will find for this dirty job. An even smaller-diameter disc (4-inch or 5-inch) will allow you to cover concave areas of the hull and to

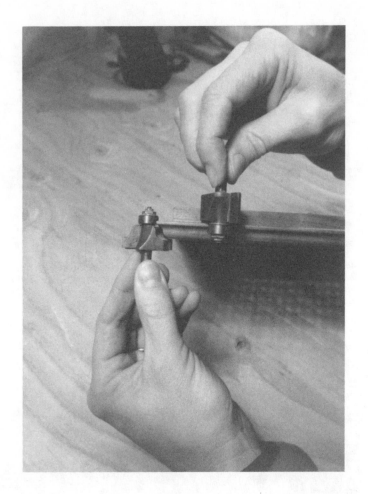

Two carbide router bits showing edge detail on a typical cabinet door. The bit on the left cuts an ogee detail, and the bit on the right cuts a ⅜-inch by ⅜-inch groove or rabbet for the back side of the door. Both have ball bearing roller guides.

reach down into the bilge and up under sheer clamp structures. It's a dirty job at best. Orbital sanders and other types of vibrating sanders provide good control and are easy to use, but their effectiveness is limited mostly to cosmetic sanding since they remove very small amounts of glass or gelcoat and tend to ride over bumps instead of removing them.

Often it is possible to avoid sanding altogether. Vigorous scraping with a sharp, steel cabinet scraper may do the job faster and much more cleanly. If the surface is relatively flat, a sharp block plane usually works well for shaving off small hairs and drips. Save sanding for a last resort, and be particularly cautious when using power equipment. Aside from the ever-present health risks from fiberglass dust, and the considerable skin irritation, there is also the danger of noise damage to the ears. OSHA-approved ear protectors are necessary even for small jobs—especially in small hulls, where noise is the worst.

Vigorous scraping with a steel cabinet scraper will usually remove drips and hairs faster and more cleanly than sanding. The scraper is normally held at a slight angle, which allows one corner to cut at each pass.

A scraper must be sharp to work. If you sharpen the scraper on all four edges, straight across, there will be eight sharp edges to use before resharpening is necessary.

Standard woodworking hand tools such as block planes, rasps, files, spokeshaves, and chisels can be used for light fiberglass work, but the blade edges will be quickly dulled and you will spend a lot of your time sharpening. Keep your best tools for finish woodworking and accumulate a group of second-string tools for glass work.

Fastening

A good epoxy glue bond is almost always superior to mechanical fastenings such as screws and bolts. Over time the metal in fastenings may corrode and leach into the surrounding glass; it may also condense water into the hole. If gluing is not practical, stainless steel self-tapping screws, or bolts of stainless steel, brass, or Monel, are the best of the mechanical fastenings for attaching hardware and decking to single-skin fiberglass hulls and decks (for illustration, see page 40). Caulking or epoxy is always recommended to maintain a good seal.

A short screw inserted into fiberglass requires a drilled pilot hole of exactly the right size—too small and the glass may crack; too large and the threads will not bite in. It pays to experiment first on a piece of scrap glass or wood. (Set a positive stop collar on the bit when the correct depth and diameter are achieved.) A drop of epoxy in the pilot hole seals and strengthens the fastening and will help to avoid trouble later. This is particularly important for critical applications such as winches, cleats, chainplates, and other hardware that will be under considerable stress.

For these critical applications, it is a sound procedure whenever possible to further reinforce the fastenings through the use of backing blocks (also commonly but inaccurately known as "butt blocks"). A backing block is a piece of wood (generally a single layer or multiple laminations of high-quality marine grade plywood) that is glued to the back side of the laminate (or embedded within the laminate) to receive and spread the stress of the fastening. More detailed information on the construction and installation of backing blocks will follow in Part II.

Patterning

The interior of a small hull is not the easiest place to work. Unlike a square room in a square house, nothing in a boat is necessarily level, square, flat, or straight-sided, and the angles can get confusing. When building or modifying small boats, the process of patterning and fitting is repeated dozens of times and often requires considerable creativity and ingenuity.

For smaller-sized projects, patterning with sheets of stiff cardboard works well. Cardboard is good patterning material for partial bulkheads, modular cabinetry, and galley build-ins—particularly countertops and other flat surfaces—but it is usually too flimsy for accurate patterning of larger items. A better solution for bunk bottoms, cabin soles, and other large, awkward shapes is to make a pattern of scrap plywood strips, which are shaped individually and then fastened together with screws or clamps. In the accompanying illustration the outboard edge of the bunk bottom was scribed and cut to fit the hull sides, then fastened to other strips to outline the length and width. Once assembled in place, the "skeleton" can be easily

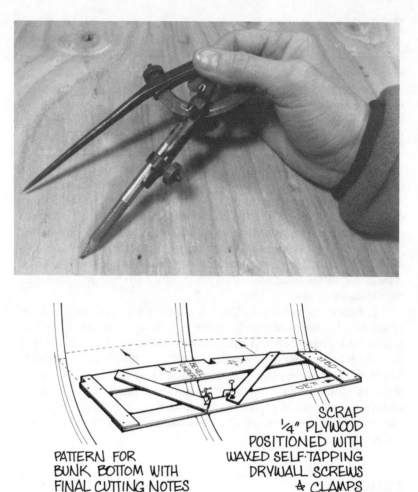

PATTERN FOR
BUNK BOTTOM WITH
FINAL CUTTING NOTES

SCRAP
¼" PLYWOOD
POSITIONED WITH
WAXED SELF·TAPPING
DRYWALL SCREWS
& CLAMPS

removed from the boat and situated on the actual piece of plywood to give an accurate tracing pattern. Notes to notch, bevel edges, or add or subtract in specific areas can be written on the pattern strips.

For patterning large bulkheads, the best solution is the traditional bulkhead patterning stick. Its construction and use will be described in detail in Part II.

Patterning large pieces of plywood is not easy, and despite your best efforts at accuracy you will probably find that further fine tuning is sometimes necessary. When modifying small boats, it seems that you're always wrestling with yet another piece of plywood—shaping, cutting a little more here and there, taking yet another shaving off the edge with a block plane to help the pieces fit properly. Patience is a large part of the job.

Working with Fiberglass and Epoxy

Fiberglass can be a mess to work with, but it does a good job, and the techniques associated with it are not difficult. Glass hulls are built up of multiple laminations of fiberglass material (cloth, mat, or roving). Each layer is saturated with resin and rolled and brushed to force out bubbles and voids so a properly bonded laminate forms. Most glass hulls have more laminations in vulnerable areas, such as the bilge and keel, and fewer laminations toward the sheer. A typical small hull might vary from ½ inch thick on the bottom to ¼ inch on the topsides, thus saving on weight where extra protection is unnecessary.

Most production glass hulls are built using a female mold, which produces a finished exterior surface. One-off hulls, which are usually custom designs, are often made from a male mold, which can produce a finished interior but requires hundreds of hours of sanding to fair the exterior, a necessary exercise but not the most pleasant way to pass your time. The best and strongest glass hulls are hand-laid, rather than built up of short glass fibers shot from a chopper gun onto the mold surface, which is the usual method for small mass-production hulls and household items such as shower stalls and tubs.

Some fiberglass hulls are formed in separate halves, laid up in port and starboard molds to allow the laminators better access to the deep and sometimes narrow bilge area. The halves are then joined using saturated fiberglass strips laid across the seam. This is usually sufficient if the seam is additionally supported by floor timbers, compartmentalization, and possibly even traditional framing. We've all heard nightmarish stories of large hulls splitting on the centerline, but fiberglass construction techniques have progressed considerably in the last few years, and many structural problems of the early years

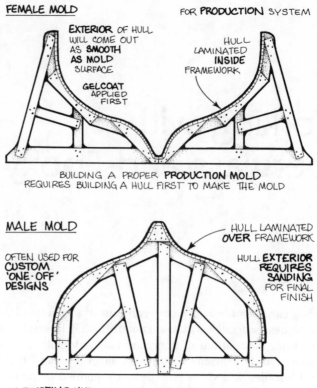

FEMALE MOLD   FOR **PRODUCTION** SYSTEM

EXTERIOR OF HULL
WILL COME OUT
AS **SMOOTH**
AS MOLD
SURFACE

HULL
LAMINATED
INSIDE
FRAMEWORK

GELCOAT
APPLIED
FIRST

BUILDING A PROPER **PRODUCTION MOLD**
REQUIRES BUILDING A HULL FIRST TO MAKE THE MOLD

MALE MOLD

HULL LAMINATED
OVER FRAMEWORK

OFTEN USED FOR
**CUSTOM
'ONE·OFF'
DESIGNS**

HULL **EXTERIOR
REQUIRES
SANDING**
FOR FINAL
FINISH

AN **EXISTING HULL** MAY BE USED FOR THIS TYPE OF MOLD

have been solved. One contributory cause of hull splitting may have been the use of steel boiler punchings, rather than lead, as internal ballast. If water somehow reaches the unsealed iron, it will start to oxidize and expand, and this may cause serious problems in time.

Components of Fiberglass Hulls

The fiberglass itself is just one component of a fiberglass hull. The other major component is polyester resin, without which the fiberglass is just so much useless fabric. Polyester resin is mixed with a catalyst to accelerate hardening, and then used to saturate the glass. When the glass turns clear, that is, when all the white opacity is gone, the material is usually completely saturated. Assuming you have mixed the resin with the correct amount of the proper catalyst, you have only to stand back and wait for it to harden. The fiberglass hull is further sealed on the exterior with gelcoat, a harder form of polyester resin with coloring added, which also provides ultraviolet (sunlight) protection.

Fiberglass

Fiberglass is available as cloth, mat, and roving, and in other more sophisticated forms such as unidirectional fibers, boards, stiff rolls, and combinations of roving and mat. All are appropriate for certain constructions, but the projects described in this book use glass in the more common cloth, mat, and roving form.

Mat is a thatch of short fibers (from one to three inches) that run in random directions. It comes in different weights, measured in ounces per square yard (or square foot) of material. The lightest and weakest we have used is similar to the webbing of an ambitious spider and, once saturated, is virtually invisible. The heaviest mat is almost as thick as a good wool blanket and takes gallons of resin and vigorous rolling to saturate properly. Mat conforms well to gradual, but complex, shapes and has approximately equal strength in all directions. Vigorous rolling will stretch and slide mat over unusual shapes.

Cloth is just what the name implies: glass fibers woven into a fabric that resembles opaque white canvas. It drapes like a fabric, is more uniform than mat, and leaves a pleasingly textured surface on exposed areas inside the hull. Like mat, it is available in various weights per square yard. We use 4-ounce, 6-ounce, 7½-ounce, and 10-ounce cloth for sheathing, repairs, and reinforcements. It may be applied in multiple layers for extra thickness and strength.

In many situations mat and cloth can be used interchangeably and alternated. Mat conforms slightly better to an irregular, rough surface and is often used as an intermediate layer between an existing glass hull and a final layer of cloth, to fill in the rough surface and provide the best bond. The many short strands of glass fiber in mat, lying as they do in all directions, conform quite easily to rough and irregular surfaces. This smoothing or flattening is not possible with glass cloth because the fibers are long and tightly woven, and they will not slide or "stretch" like mat. On the other hand, cloth is easier to control than mat, something for the first-time glasser to keep in mind. Saturated mat can split into uncontrollable fragments that stick to everything, especially resin-sticky hands or gloves. Cloth can be gently tugged into shape on the hull or mold, whereas mat will shred into pieces if you try to pull it into place. For this reason—plus the fact that multiple layers of cloth usually result in a better resin-to-fiberglass ratio—small hulls are often laminated entirely out of cloth. Cloth is also best for sheathing, and like all glass, it improves the abrasion resistance of wood.

Woven *roving* is a much heavier weave than standard cloth, with bulky strands similar to burlap and even thicker. Roving will not conform as easily as other lighter types of glass to tight curves and complex shapes, but it adds tremendous strength in flatter areas. It also adds considerable weight because it requires more resin for saturation. Large hulls use roving between layers of mat to build up

Fiberglass mat: a thatch of glass fibers in random directions. Mat can be rolled and spread or stippled with a brush, and it conforms to uneven surfaces more easily than cloth. The fibers can be separated by gentle pulling, and pieces can be added as needed. Mat will also shred easily when handled by resin-sticky gloves.

required thickness, the mat serving as a lighter sandwich material to improve adhesion and provide consistent strength.

Mat, cloth, and heavier roving result in distinct types of finished surfaces. When properly saturated and rolled, mat leaves a utilitarian surface that is not unattractive as long as it is in keeping with the type of boat and matches the surrounding glass work. Drips and loose hairs should be carefully flattened and spread with the roller or they will stick out, especially if the surface is eventually painted. Roving leaves a much rougher surface that is seldom left exposed except in very rough workboats or cheaper hulls. Cloth leaves the most consistent and finished-looking surface, which looks good either natural or painted and also blends well with the woodwork inside a hull. Properly saturated and rolled, none of these surfaces should require extensive sanding, although sometimes a light scraping with a sharp cabinet scraper will be needed to remove dust craters and small bubbles. There is little or no difference in the final appearance of a polyester or epoxy resin surface.

The number and weight-per-square-yard of fiberglass layers required for a glassing operation depend on the hull thickness, the shape of the hull, and whether the hull is single skin, sandwich construction, or reinforcement over wood. A typical layup schedule for reinforcing the interior of a small glass hull of approximately ¼-inch

Roving has a much heavier weave than mat or cloth and adds tremendous strength—and considerable weight—to flatter areas.

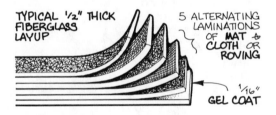

thickness might begin with a thin- or medium-weight layer of mat to obtain the best possible bond to the hull. Then, while the mat is still wet, additional layers can be added, perhaps alternating with layers of cloth. For heavy-duty reinforcement, you might want to add a layer of lightweight roving sandwiched between a layer of mat on either side, and end up with a layer of cloth for a pleasing finished surface. The entire operation should add up to approximately ⅛ inch of additional hull thickness.

For sheathing over wood, 4-ounce or 6-ounce glass is generally appropriate and will become transparent when saturated. If transparency and natural finish are not factors, 9-ounce or 10-ounce cloth adds considerable protection and can also be doubled or tripled for considerable additional strength.

Six-ounce fiberglass cloth tape, in 1½-inch and 3-inch widths. Tape does not shred like mat, and its selvage edges make it easy to work with. It can be used for outside and inside corners and over fillets, or applied in multiple layers for additional support.

SPREAD **THICKENED EPOXY** WITH A WIDE **PUTTY KNIFE** TO FAIR MULTIPLE LAYERS OF **FIBERGLASS TAPE** ON OUTSIDE OF CORNER

SECTION
THROUGH TRANSOM
OR CABIN TOP CORNER

Glass Tape. Glass tape is a particularly useful form of fiberglass, with a number of applications on boats. Available in various weights and in various widths from 2-inch to 6-inch, it can be wrapped around corners and even spiraled around masts and spars, oars, and boat-hooks. It has a bound selvage edge that will not ravel and shred (as will glass cloth cut into strips), and it can be positioned by tugging on the ends to make it conform to unusual shapes and to help smooth out wrinkles. Glass tape is quite useful on outside corners, such as

WORKING WITH THE
MATERIALS
24

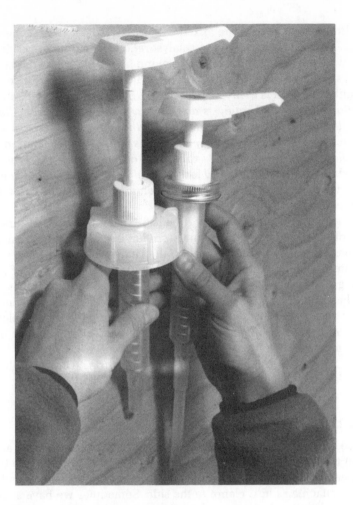

These epoxy "mini-pumps" are inserted into epoxy containers to provide the correct metering of epoxy resin with catalyst. Much less expensive than more complicated types of pumps, they are quite suitable for the occasional epoxy user.

along the front and back edges of cabins. It is also quite useful on inside corners, where it adds surprising strength to vulnerable joints. It is also often applied over epoxy fillets or concave moldings.

Resin

Various types and brands of resins are on the market, including polyesters, vinylesters, improved polyesters, epoxies, and others. Plain polyester serves well for some less critical projects, because that is probably what your production boat was built with in the first place. Epoxy resin is about twice as expensive as polyester, but its superior bonding ability makes it the resin of choice for certain critical repair and reinforcing operations on the glass hull. (Polyester resin was never intended to be a glue.) Epoxy also seals the surface of the fiberglass laminate much more effectively than polyester resin, providing a superior moisture barrier.

Both types of resins are mixed with a catalyst to accelerate hardening. With epoxy, the resin-to-catalyst ratio is usually more critical than with polyester, and a metering pump (available from your supplier) should be used to ensure accuracy. Polyester catalyst for small quantities of resin is easily dispensed in drops from a squeeze bottle. *Caution: Resins and catalysts are toxic and corrosive. Never allow them to touch your skin, and make sure that your work area is adequately ventilated. The same precautions apply to solvents used in fiberglass work. Acetone, for example, is absorbed directly through the skin and can have harmful long-term effects, so you should never wash your hands in it, as was once common practice in many fiberglass boatyards.*

Temperature and humidity (to a lesser extent) affect the curing time of catalyzed resins. Beginners are advised to start with small batches until they are familiar with the characteristics of the resin, the effects of temperature, and the amount of catalyst needed. If the resin gets warm and begins to gel as you work, it's best to set it aside and begin with a fresh, smaller portion of resin in a new container. When the air is cool and the sun not yet up, we might start with eight drops of catalyst to a one-pound coffee can half full of resin; as the day warms—along with the resin, fiberglass, and work surface—we might reduce the catalyst to six or even four drops. Direct sunlight on a flat surface can cause rapid acceleration of the cure time.

Tools for Glassing

Coffee cans make good glassing containers. They're easy to clean and about the right size for small jobs, and they're easy to carry into the forepeak or down into a tight bilge. We often cut a plywood handle or just attach an old C clamp to the side. Sometimes we have small batches in half a dozen cans around when working in hot weather,

MIXING CANS WITH 'C' CLAMPS & PLYWOOD HANDLES

because previously mixed batches must kick (catalyze) before you dump them. You can also use plastic mix cups; easily and cheaply available.

Jobs always go easiest if all the tools are at hand, so the organized glasser should have ready:

- scrapers for preparing the surface
- inexpensive or disposable brushes for saturating and stippling
- roller handles and foam refills for resin application
- paint pan for reloading foam rollers with resin
- plastic or aluminum slotted roller for rolling out bubbles, excess resin, and voids and for spreading and smoothing overlaps
- old coffee cans or other mixing containers
- squeegees for spreading resin and removing drips
- stapler or duct tape for holding glass in place on vertical or overhead surfaces
- respirator for glass dust if sanding is necessary (If you absolutely *must* spend a lot of time glassing in a small enclosed space, a positive pressure respirator should be used.)
- fan for ventilation when working indoors or inside a hull
- scissors (for cutting mat or cloth)
- shears (for cutting roving)
- razor knife with extra blades
- straightedge for cutting guide
- surgical or dishwashing gloves
- mixing sticks (tongue depressors do nicely)
- barrier cream for all exposed skin
- old clothes for glassing (flannel or cotton is best)

The Glassing Operation
If you've never glassed before, try a small sample piece before you jump into a complicated project. Make your mistakes on a surfboard, or an old Corvette, or your shower stall, not on the boat.

Surface Preparation
If you intend to laminate new glass onto a hull interior—the principal fiberglassing operation called for in this book—start by washing the area with detergent or a solvent, to remove wax. Then run your hand over the surface to make sure there are no wild hairs or drips that will hold your first layer of glass off the surface, thus preventing a good bond. If there are, try to remove them by scraping rather than sanding. Another technique for smoothing is to partially fill the rough surface of the laminate with a thickened mixture of epoxy and microballoons (see ahead, under Fillets). This mixture may be troweled

on or applied with a flexible squeegee; the first layer of fiberglass is then applied to the still-wet surface. When building up layers of glass, the individual pieces should be divided into sizes that are easy to handle. With fiberglass it makes little difference whether the pieces are laid vertically, horizontally, or diagonally; the strength is approximately equal in all directions. Overlaps of approximately two inches will provide consistent strength to the layup for all but perhaps the thickest roving, which might need slightly wider overlaps. Thick overlaps are easily smoothed and spread over a slightly larger area with a slotted plastic roller, and successive overlaps can be staggered or placed at different locations to prevent a thick buildup in any one location.

Saturating the Glass

There are two good methods for saturating glass with resin: you can saturate the glass and then position it on the boat (the so-called wet method), or you can position it on the boat first and then apply the resin. This latter technique, the so-called dry method, is considered easier for first-timers because positioning can be accomplished without the additional pressures of dealing with wet resin and saturated cloth. But if you're working in cramped space inside the hull, the wet method may be your best choice (the compensating factor is that it gives a slightly better bond). Since a large, wet piece of glass is difficult to move around once it touches the hull surface, you might want to consider cutting smaller strips and overlapping them slightly. Fold the piece to carry it into the hull; then unfold it onto the surface.

Wet Method. Start by rolling or brushing a coat of catalyzed resin on the target area to ensure a good bond. Then do all the preliminary saturating of the glass outside the boat. Lay the cut glass on a piece of clean cardboard on a bench or other flat work surface, and apply the resin. Continue until you can almost see through the glass to the surface below or until the glass is uniformly opaque. Cloth is quite easy to saturate with a roller, but mat requires care to keep it from shredding. Soft foam rollers cut to appropriate lengths work well for saturating lightweight mat. Roving requires energetic stippling (jabbing motions) with a brush to saturate the thick fibers and force it into place without voids.

Once you get the glass saturated and positioned on the surface to be covered, you can begin to work it down. For a proper bond it is quite important not to leave voids caused by small holes, bubbles, or depressions in the surface. Bonding a layer of mat in place usually involves stippling with a brush, followed (if the surface areas to be covered permit it) by rolling with a hard or soft roller to mold the mat to the surface. Soft foam rollers work well with lightweight mat; a slotted plastic roller works best when applying a heavy layer or multiple layers of mat over a rough surface. The slotted roller will

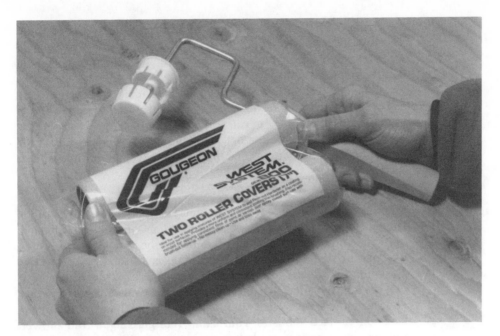

Foam-covered epoxy rollers and roller handle. Rollers may be cut into short sections for working on small areas.

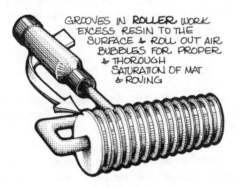

GROOVES IN **ROLLER** WORK EXCESS RESIN TO THE SURFACE & ROLL OUT AIR BUBBLES FOR PROPER & THOROUGH SATURATION OF MAT & ROVING

remove bubbles and bring excess resin to the surface, to be picked up by a foam roller or brush. When bonding mat to a rough surface, repeated rolling will actually separate some of the glass fibers and allow them to be moved around to fill low spots.

Dry Method. For this application method, roll resin over the target spot to help saturate the glass from behind and to help hold it in place. Position the glass using staples* or masking tape, if needed, especially on overhead surfaces (once saturated it will stick easily). Pour or roll resin over the cloth, using a roller to achieve uniform

---

* With a good staple gun and a good, strong grip, staples can often be driven into fiberglass—deep enough, at least, to hold a cloth strip temporarily in position.

saturation. Remove tape as you work, but staples may be left until the resin kicks, then taken out later. Sometimes we feel as though we're hanging wallpaper underwater, but the process works—if you're organized.

Whether you work wet or dry, it's a decided advantage if you can complete an entire section of laminating in one session. By adding layers while the surface is still wet, you eliminate the need for additional surface preparation between layers, thus saving yourself tedious sanding or scraping. The bond is usually superior as well.

The "Itch Factor"

Fiberglass is notorious for making you feel itchy, and those with a tendency toward allergies and skin problems usually are affected more than others. We've already mentioned the importance of avoiding sanding fiberglass if at all possible, because sanding breaks the glass into tiny floating pieces that get on your skin, no matter how you dress. If you plan on extensive glassing, it usually helps to forego your morning shower, and possibly your shower the night before, to leave the protective oils on your skin. After glassing, a cold shower followed by a hot one (or better yet, a sauna) with a cold rinse will do as good a job as can be expected. When you finish glassing, throw your clothes away. If you *must* keep them for your next glassing project, don't wash them with your other clothes or you may find that these become itchy also.

Fillets

A fillet is a concave or triangular strip of thickened epoxy that is used to attach, seal, waterproof, and reinforce bulkheads, gussets, panels, transoms, and other items on a boat. Fillets conform to almost any fixed or changing angle and can be applied overhead as well as on vertical or horizontal surfaces. They spread stress over a larger area and can provide impressive strength, while giving a finished appearance.

A fillet consists of epoxy resin and a catalyst, mixed with a filler

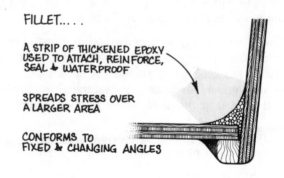

FILLET.....

A STRIP OF THICKENED EPOXY USED TO ATTACH, REINFORCE, SEAL & WATERPROOF

SPREADS STRESS OVER A LARGER AREA

CONFORMS TO FIXED & CHANGING ANGLES

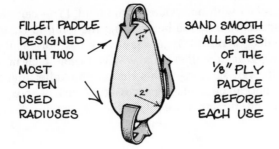

FILLET PADDLE DESIGNED WITH TWO MOST OFTEN USED RADIUSES

SAND SMOOTH ALL EDGES OF THE 1/8" PLY PADDLE BEFORE EACH USE

1"

2"

to provide the desired consistency and strength. (Don't make fillets out of polyester resin; these will shrink, swell, and crack.) The two most common fillers are colloidal silica and microballoons. Both are generally available from boatbuilding supply houses as well as from many epoxy suppliers. Which filler you use depends on the goal you have in mind. Colloidal silica is a high-strength mixture, but it is also very dense and heavy and nearly impossible to sand once the resin has cured. Microballoons form a lighter filleting mixture that can be sanded easily and works well for cosmetic applications. The two fillers can also be mixed in various proportions to create the balance of high strength and low weight appropriate for the application at hand, or you can buy premixed fillers, available under various trade names. The idea is to build a fillet consistent with the strength and scantlings of surrounding structural members.

It takes experimentation as well to arrive at the appropriate filler-to-resin ratio. Too loose and the fillet will run and sag; too thick and it will be difficult to spread and sand and may not bond well. The temperature of the resin affects the filler-to-resin ratio—an important consideration when working in hot weather. Small batches are more manageable, allowing a better control of the mixture and providing time to apply, shape, and clean up the fillet before the epoxy kicks.

When applying a fillet, it's helpful to have a fillet paddle, made to the appropriate radius. Start by applying the fillet mixture to the joint area with a putty knife or mixing stick. Follow with the paddle, working short sections at a time and pulling, not pushing, the paddle

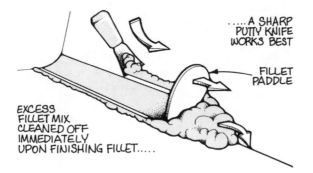

.....A SHARP PUTTY KNIFE WORKS BEST

FILLET PADDLE

EXCESS FILLET MIX CLEANED OFF IMMEDIATELY UPON FINISHING FILLET.....

along in contact with both sides of the joint. (You can also slide a bottle or squeegee over the bead, along the joint, to achieve much the same effect; a gloved finger may work best for small sizes and tight places.) When the fillet is the way you want it, clean the excess from the edges by scraping with a sharp putty knife; after the epoxy kicks, the fillet can be sanded as necessary. A coat of epoxy resin will further seal and strengthen the fillet, as well as making it easy to clean or paint.

Part II
Structural Reinforcements for Fiberglass Sailboats

Safety First

Production fiberglass boats are standardized versions of stock designs, built to take advantage of production line techniques. To remain viable in the competitive world of corporate boatbuilding, where many operations are more apt to be controlled by accountants than boatbuilders, a few corners may get cut. Glaring defects are fortunately rare (although some builders and certain designs develop reputations for specific weaknesses), but there's no doubt that boats aren't built in the same manner that they once were, and the changes are not always in the best interest of the boats. Not too many years ago you seldom or never saw a rivet on a boat; they were considered poor fastenings at best. Now they are all too common. Even if the fastenings are adequate, there may not be enough of them to do the job, or they may lack proper backing blocks and washers. It's a little too easy to skip a few laminations of fiberglass, or to do a less than perfect job rolling out each lamination. Even the simple task of measuring out each batch of resin and mixing the proper amount of catalyst can get shortchanged under the pressures of production boatbuilding. A bulkhead may be too thin or poorly braced to provide adequate support for a deck-stepped mast or the necessary stiffness to a section of thin glass hull. Rigging might be cheap imported wire made of low-quality alloys, which looks great until it gets wet and rusts. It's all fine for a calm day on the bay, but offshore in rough weather it could be disastrous. Misgivings about the strength and consistency of construction can put a definite crimp in your boating style. The defects may turn out to be just minor, a few small things, but all together they can prevent you from dropping the mooring and heading out for points unknown. So for peace of mind as well as for safety, it is worth the time and effort to go through a process of systematically strengthening the boat, paying special attention to vul-

The Liner Problem

Many production boatbuilders now make extensive use of hull liners (sometimes known as hull "socks") which are inserted into the hull before the deck is installed to provide an instant interior. Liners are usually attached somewhere near the hull-to-deck joint either by mechanical fastenings, such as screws or bolts, or with mastic. The bottom of the liner may "float" in the hull, or it may be attached with fiberglass tabs. Liners are primarily a cost-saving device for the builder, since they can be built in molds and installed by unskilled labor. Like the hull itself, they are made of polyester resin and fiberglass, hand laid or shot onto the mold surface through a pressurized chopper gun. They are usually gel-coated on the exposed surface to provide a finished, easy-to-clean surface, similar in many ways to a molded fiberglass shower stall.

Liners vary in size and complexity and usually contain a number of interior components such as cabin sole, bulkheads, and cabinetry. On larger boats there may be separate liners for individual compartments, but on small boats the liner is likely to be a one-piece unit, filling the entire hull from bow to transom. While adding some strength and stiffness to the hull, they also waste considerable cabin space. The major disadvantage, however, is that they cover the inside surface of the hull, which can make repairs of any kind, and even routine maintenance, very complicated. For emergency hull repairs a liner is a nightmare because it prevents ready access to the hull itself, and it may hide the true extent of the damage.

If you are forced to cut into or remove a section of hull liner to make repairs or modifications, take comfort in the fact that by making critical surfaces and hardware attachments ac-

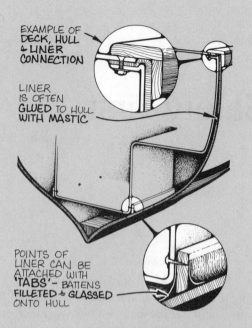

EXAMPLE OF **DECK, HULL & LINER** CONNECTION

LINER IS OFTEN GLUED TO HULL WITH MASTIC

POINTS OF LINER CAN BE ATTACHED WITH 'TABS' – BATTENS FILLETED & GLASSED ONTO HULL

cessible, you are adding significantly to the seaworthiness of your boat. Depending on the type of modifications you are making, you may be able to get by without removing the entire liner. Small cutouts, for access to critical hardware such as chainplates, cleats, bow eyes, etc., can be fitted with inspection plates for future ease of access. If a larger section of the liner must be removed, it is sometimes possible to locate a partial or complete bulkhead to serve as a natural termination point for the remaining liner. The bulkhead is attached with an epoxy fillet; then the liner is butted against the bulkhead or attached with another fillet. However you work it out, there's no getting around the fact that liners make for a lot of extra work, turning small jobs into big ones and routine maintenance into full-fledged retrofits.

nerable areas. The problems considered in this section are common to many types of fiberglass boats, from solo canoes to world cruisers. The solutions vary considerably in complexity, from easy weekend projects to major retrofits. But jobs can be tackled one at a time and sequenced from minor to more ambitious as you gain skill and confidence.

Chainplates and Hardware Problems

On small, marconi-rigged sailboats, particularly those with deck-stepped masts, the standing rigging must endure considerable stress. Most standing rigging failures occur at terminals and attachment points, where a great deal of force is concentrated in a small area. It's all too easy over a period of time to take a few extra turns on a turnbuckle and put whopping stress on the entire system. The same potentially dangerous combination—considerable force concentrated in a small area—applies to other critical hardware such as deck cleats, chocks, bow eyes, and rudder hardware attachments. Problems can occur either from stress fractures in the hardware itself or from inadequate fastening and bedding.

Stress Fractures

Stress fractures in metal castings of any type are suspect, particularly when the item in question must carry a heavy load. The fracture may be no more than a hairline crack, barely visible except with a strong magnifying glass, or it may be obvious from the corrosion stain down the side of the hull. Either way, replacement is in order.

Be careful what you buy! Quality marine hardware is usually quite dependable, but cheap imported castings of inferior grades are everywhere, and it's often difficult to tell the difference until the hardware has been on the boat for awhile. Stay away from aluminum, chrome, and brass castings of unknown origin and stick with old reliables like silicone bronze and good stainless steel from reputable suppliers who guarantee their products.

Bedding and Fastening Problems

More often than not, chainplate and hardware problems are the result of improper bedding and fastening. A good flexible bedding is necessary for all hardware attachments, and the bedding must retain its elasticity over the years to remain effective. Hardware exposed to heavy pulling or jerking loads can separate from cheap or inadequate bedding, especially if the backing blocks and fastenings are inadequate, allowing salt and water into the cracks to encourage corrosion and watersoak in critical areas that need all their strength. It is all too common to find small glass hulls that have no backing blocks at all behind and around their chainplates and stay bolts—only a small, inadequate bead of bedding that soon starts to leak as the bedding hardens.

The solution is straightforward, though not always easy to execute. Chainplates, forestay and backstay fittings, and all other critical hardware attached to the hull or deck need to be well fastened, with the stress points spread over as large an area as is practical. Generally this goal breaks out as a four-step operation:

- removing old bolts and fastenings
- repairing worn or watersoaked laminate around the bolt holes
- installing effective backing blocks
- redrilling, rebedding, and refastening

If your boat has strap-type chainplates, a prime remedy for chainplate problems is to replace the straps with longer ones that reach farther around the hull. This not only spreads the stress over a larger area but allows you to increase the number of fastenings as well. To a certain extent this strategy can also be applied to cleats, chocks, and other hardware, but it makes sense only if the fitting in question is undersize to begin with. Replacing a fitting with one that is far larger and sturdier than the surrounding construction is needless overkill—and useless additional weight. Scantlings should be as consistent as possible throughout.

Removing the Old Bolts

Access is often the biggest problem when dealing with hardware retrofits. Shrouds are usually accessible by removing some furniture inside the hull.* Forestay and backstay hardware, cleats, chocks, and bow eyes may require additional work to gain access, and may even require cutting into the hull. Sometimes just getting a hand or an arm into a small locker will be enough to remove nuts from bolts; in these situations Vise-Grips are usually the tool of choice for holding or

---

* Repairs to shroud chainplates can often be done with the mast still in place by tying the shrouds off temporarily to lifelines or deck fittings while you work on one side at a time.

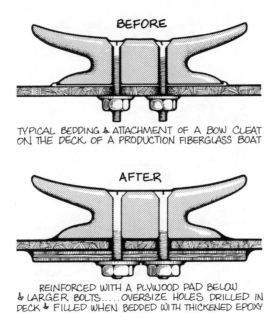

BEFORE

TYPICAL BEDDING & ATTACHMENT OF A BOW CLEAT
ON THE DECK OF A PRODUCTION FIBERGLASS BOAT

AFTER

REINFORCED WITH A PLYWOOD PAD BELOW
& LARGER BOLTS.....OVERSIZE HOLES DRILLED IN
DECK & FILLED WHEN BEDDED WITH THICKENED EPOXY

loosening the nut. A short ratchet can also be handy; for carriage bolts you may need a helper pushing on the head of the bolt from outside. If you must cut into the hull or hull liner to gain access, make the hole as small and out of the way as possible and take comfort in the fact that you can repair almost anything on a glass hull better than new with epoxy and a little elbow grease.

Repairing the Laminate

Once the bolts are removed, carefully inspect the area around the bolt holes to determine the health of the laminate. Healthy fiberglass makes a clear, sharp sound when you rap it, or sometimes a high-pitched ring when you cut through it. If you hear a dull thud, or if the laminate feels soft and mushy or shows obvious corrosion stains, there is probably watersoak damage, and the weakened laminate should be reinforced or replaced. Dry the area, remove the damaged laminate if necessary, and build up new layers of cloth or mat, making sure to lap them generously onto healthy sections of the hull. (If you're new to glass work, refer to Part I, "Working with Fiberglass and Epoxy.")

If the damage to the laminate is minimal—all you really need is some filling and patching around the bolt holes—epoxy is ideal for these minor repairs. It not only fills in the holes but greatly increases the holding power of the fastening. In fact, our standard procedure, on new work as well as old, is to drill our holes slightly oversize and fill in with epoxy. For example, for a ½-inch carriage bolt, we might drill a ⅝-inch or even a ¾-inch hole and make a 1/16-inch (or ⅛-inch)

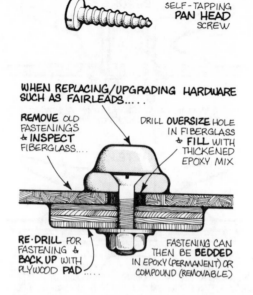

SELF-TAPPING
PAN HEAD
SCREW

WHEN REPLACING/UPGRADING HARDWARE
SUCH AS FAIRLEADS.....

REMOVE OLD
FASTENINGS
& INSPECT
FIBERGLASS....

DRILL OVERSIZE HOLE
IN FIBERGLASS
& FILL WITH
THICKENED
EPOXY MIX

RE·DRILL FOR
FASTENING &
BACK UP WITH
PLYWOOD PAD.....

FASTENING CAN
THEN BE BEDDED
IN EPOXY (PERMANENT) OR
COMPOUND (REMOVABLE)

epoxy "collar." The bolt can be inserted while the epoxy is still wet, but neater results are obtained by allowing the epoxy to kick and then inserting the bolt. If maximum holding power is your goal (and the bolt will not subsequently need to be removed), you can slather the hole, and the bolt itself, with a thin coat of epoxy at the time of insertion.

In certain situations the best approach may be to fill in the old bolt holes and drill new ones. This will probably be the case if you are replacing a fitting with a larger one, or repositioning an old one slightly so that the holes no longer match up. Once again, epoxy is ideal for the job, and it can be used either thickened or unthickened.* Unthickened epoxy provides the maximum sealing and saturation, but if the bolt holes are overhead or on a vertical surface, you may need to thicken with silica and/or microballoons to keep the mixture from oozing out of the holes.

Installing Backing Blocks

Once repair work to the laminate is complete, you can move ahead to attaching backing blocks. The blocks should be made of hardwood or AA marine grade plywood soaked in epoxy, and they should be large enough to spread strain over a wide area. The method of installation will vary from situation to situation and is usually obvious. The accompanying illustrations show typical installations for externally and internally mounted chainplates.

---

* If the hole to be filled is a large one—more than ½ inch in diameter, or 3 or 4 inches deep—it is probably best to plug it with a hardwood dowel held in place with epoxy rather than using epoxy for the entire filling.

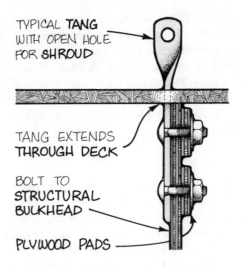

TYPICAL **TANG** WITH OPEN HOLE FOR **SHROUD**

TANG EXTENDS **THROUGH DECK**

BOLT TO **STRUCTURAL BULKHEAD**

PLYWOOD PADS

The attachment of blocks is usually best done in one step, but if there is extreme curvature to the hull it may be necessary to use two or three laminations of thinner plywood to allow the block to bend more easily without deforming the hull shape. If the backing blocks are visible, you may want to radius the edges with a block plane or router. The top edge should be sealed with epoxy and shaped to allow run-off of water.

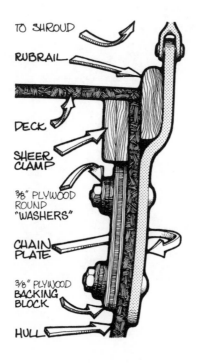

TO SHROUD

RUBRAIL

DECK

SHEER CLAMP

⅜" PLYWOOD ROUND "WASHERS"

CHAIN PLATE

⅜" PLYWOOD BACKING BLOCK

HULL

Compression Pads. Foam-sandwich, honeycomb-core, and balsa-core hulls and decks require solid compression pads for hardware fastenings; otherwise the area around the fastening is likely to crumple like an aluminum beer can. Some builders advise solid fiberglass for compression pads, but quality solid-core plywood is just as good and a lot less work. To install a compression pad, remove the core material around the fastening and epoxy a pad of plywood in place, sealing everything, including the bolt holes, with epoxy.

Bedding

Hardware should never be laid against bare fiberglass or bare wood without a good elastic bedding. Our own first choice for bedding material in most situations is epoxy, because the WEST System epoxy we use has adequate flexibility (some epoxy formulations are too brittle), along with epoxy's superior bonding and waterproofing capacities. If you choose not to use epoxy, there is a variety of good marine bedding compounds on the market, readily available at marine hardware stores. Bedding compounds are good when sealing large gaps, when maximum flexibility is required, or when the hardware requires occasional removal.

Bedding compound should be applied thickly enough so that when you tighten down on the fastening, some squeezes out along the sides (but don't overtighten so that the entire bed squeezes out). Bolt holes can still be sealed with a liberal dose of epoxy to prevent future watersoak damage to the laminate.

Hull Reinforcements

Hull-to-Deck Connections

The perimeter flange that mates a one-piece glass deck to the hull can be a vulnerable area on many production glass boats. A flange need not entail great design complexity—in simplest form it is merely a straightforward shelf—but to work well it must be properly fastened and caulked. Polyester resin shrinks and swells with the temperature and humidity, with the result that a one-piece, 30-foot glass deck might expand and contract as much as two inches during the course of a hot day and cold night. This puts a great amount of stress on the connection and demands more elasticity than some types of caulking provide, especially over the long haul. As the caulking starts to fail, the hull-to-deck flange can produce a plethora of mysterious leaks that are tricky to find. Water entering up near the bow, in the form of spray, can sometimes migrate along the length of the flange to leak over a quarter berth aft. The spot may leak only on a certain tack, or under certain conditions of loading and temperature. Such small leaks have been known to drive people to fits, especially if the leak is over your bunk.

Sometimes about the best you can do for such leaks is to recaulk along the length of the seam, following up as needed with a close regular pattern of additional fastenings. Unfortunately, because of deck overlays, caprails, and rubrails, you can't always get to the seam to apply the caulking. With some types of boats it may be possible, using small hardwood wedges, to force the joint open just enough to insert the tip of a caulking tube. (Warming the tube before the job will make the caulk flow more easily, and a warm day is better for the job than a cold one.) Removing a molding or rubrail may provide access, but sometimes the only alternative is to approach from the

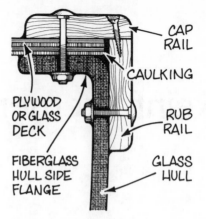

GLASS HULL TO-DECK JOINT

CAP RAIL

CAULKING

PLYWOOD OR GLASS DECK

RUB RAIL

FIBERGLASS HULL SIDE FLANGE

GLASS HULL

inside—a hard, dirty job that often requires the removal of furniture and headliners.

An even more important concern than leaks is the overall strength of the connection itself. Although we ourselves have never heard of a deck coming off a hull, we have seen some sloppy and obviously poor flange connections using inadequate fastenings (such as rivets) or an inadequate number of fastenings. If rivets are accessible, they can sometimes be removed and replaced; if not, they can be left in place and sturdier fastenings (self-tapping screws, or better yet, bolts) fitted alongside. Access permitting, the best fastenings are stainless steel or bronze carriage bolts, or machine screws with nuts, backed up on the underside by a washer at the very least and preferably by a thin plywood backing block. If access to the underside is a problem, machine or cap screws, liberally coated with epoxy, provide good localized holding power. Spacing will vary with the size and type of fastening used, but a typical pattern for a small (20- to 30-foot) hull might be $\frac{1}{4}$-inch carriage bolts every four to six inches. Most types of connections can be further improved and sealed by building a caprail/rubrail combination that overlaps the joints, as in the accompanying illustration. Handrail stanchions can also be used to advantage to reinforce this joint in specific areas.

Some small hulls need additional stiffening to prevent unusual flexing, which causes caulking to break loose. The installation of knees, bulkheads, and other stiffening devices will be discussed later in this section.

Oil Canning

If you've ever used one of those old oil cans that works by squeezing the bottom while you hold it upside down, you'll know immediately why this term applies to fiberglass hulls. It's a slight puffing or panting, more than the normal working of the hull, which usually only shows up when underway. While generally most pronounced in the forepeak area and in a head sea, it can happen on any weak or unsupported area of the hull, including the bilge, a broad transom, or a minimally supported bottom of a motorboat. If left uncorrected, it can lead to fatigue of the laminate and a premature deterioration of the boat—and in the worst case scenario, a sudden failure in rough conditions.

Oil canning is a clue that the hull needs additional bracing or stiffening. There are two solutions: You can increase the thickness of the hull in affected areas by simply adding more laminations to the inside, or you can provide a specific stiffener like a rib or a partial bulkhead. Specific reinforcements usually save weight but are sometimes more time consuming to design and install.

Building Up the Laminate

If the vulnerable area is easily accessible and weight is not a problem, it is a simple matter to add additional layers to the laminate, following the procedure described in Part I under "Working with Fiberglass and Epoxy." A typical interior reinforcement for a small boat might consist of a layer of mat, followed by a layer of 6-ounce cloth, followed by another layer of mat, and ending up with a layer of cloth to leave a finished surface. Be sure to give adequate attention to surface preparation, avoiding sanding whenever possible by scraping and filling.

Building up additional laminations is also an accepted remedy for foam-sandwich or balsa-core hulls that have been damaged or are suffering from isolated areas of watersoak. Starting from the inside, dig out all the affected foam or balsa; then replace the area with new laminations of mat and/or cloth, saturated with epoxy (rather than polyester) for a waterproof seal.

Adding Stiffeners

In addition to (or in place of) building up the laminate, you can add specific stiffeners as needed. The "mailing tube ribs" pictured here add a remarkable amount of stiffening with little additional weight. Since the half rounds themselves are basically nonstructural, merely serving as a form for the fiberglass, they can be made out of lightweight materials: cardboard mailing tubes cut in half, or rolls or blocks of foam shaped to a cylindrical form. If you use foam, bear in mind that it must be compatible with the resin you're working with; a test piece is advisable before starting a big job.

The first step is to cut the cardboard or foam tube in half, using scissors or a band saw. If necessary, small kerf cuts can be made in the back side to allow the tube or half round to conform more easily to the shape of the hull. Position the tube in the intended area and

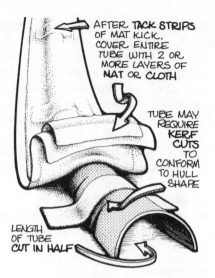

AFTER TACK STRIPS OF MAT KICK, COVER ENTIRE TUBE WITH 2 OR MORE LAYERS OF MAT OR CLOTH

TUBE MAY REQUIRE KERF CUTS TO CONFORM TO HULL SHAPE

LENGTH OF TUBE CUT IN HALF

brace it somehow, or use masking tape or duct tape to hold it temporarily in place until it is glassed.

These stiffeners do not have to be placed exactly parallel or perpendicular to the waterline of the boat. In fact, it's often advantageous, particularly in the forepeak, to place the ribbing at right angles to the stem angle. As the stem angle changes from the forepeak to the tip of the bow, the angle of the ribs also changes according to their position. In traditional boatbuilding this is known as a cant frame, and its changing angle provides optimum bracing of the forepeak area. The only drawback, perhaps, is that it does not look as "traditional" as vertical ribs, or stringers aligned parallel to the waterline.*

Once the half rounds are positioned, place a number of small tack strips of cloth or mat over each rib, lapping well onto the hull on either side. These strips should be saturated with catalyzed resin before placement and stippled gently with a soft brush to ensure the proper bond. (Either polyester or epoxy resin may be used for this operation, but epoxy is recommended for its superior bond.) As soon as there are enough strips in place to hold the half round onto the hull once the resin kicks, leave the tube alone. Don't pester it or try to begin wrapping additional layers of glass until the tack strips are hard.

When the resin has cured, remove the bracing or masking tape, and glass the tube firmly in place with two or three laminations of mat, perhaps topping it all off with a layer of 6-ounce cloth to leave a nice finished surface. You may wish to add a small fillet on each

---

* While you're up in the forepeak, you may want to check out the hull centerline from the waterline down to the keel because that's where you'll most likely take the impact if you hit something floating in the water. It's quite simple to add a few additional layers to the laminate if that will make you feel better about those things that go bump in the middle of the night.

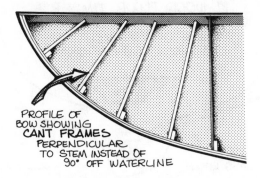

PROFILE OF
BOW SHOWING
CANT FRAMES
PERPENDICULAR
TO STEM INSTEAD OF
90° OFF WATERLINE

side of the tube to support the glass even better. If you do a clean job of laminating and take pains to match the port and starboard sides, the stiffening ribs won't look as sloppy as you might imagine. A coat of paint makes them look even more finished and integrated with the hull.

Floor Timber and Bilge Area

The floor timber and bilge area is particularly critical in deep-keel sailboats with either internal or external ballast. This area is the fulcrum of balance between the ballast and form stability of the boat's hull and the driving force of its sails. Imagine the whopping strains down in the bilge in a heavily ballasted hull resisting a full press of sail in rough water! Wood boatbuilders give this area special attention, but glass builders sometimes neglect it. Because glass laminate is so easy to form to curving shapes, it's easy to forget that the structure may need additional bracing.

The bilge area is also susceptible to water absorption. The bilges of many boats are perpetually wet, with stuffing boxes, through-hull leaks, condensation, and spray all contributing to the ever-present gallon of water sloshing around down below. Exterior hull surfaces are sealed with gelcoat for protection, but interior surfaces are normally left unprotected, and over time the unprotected polyester resin in the bilge area will absorb small amounts of water, which may eventually weaken the laminate in this critical area.

This problem has a straightforward solution. Two or three coats of epoxy resin will seal the bilge area and provide a much improved moisture barrier, plus a degree of improved abrasion resistance. When applying epoxy resin over polyester resin, the only requirements are to dry the area thoroughly, with fan and heater if necessary, and to make sure the surface is clean. Since epoxy is sensitive to ultraviolet light, one additional consideration for a small, undecked hull is to protect the bilge area from direct sunlight, or to protect the epoxy by applying a coat of paint.

If the strength of the bilge is suspect, additional structural measures must be considered. The simple ploy of adding laminations to

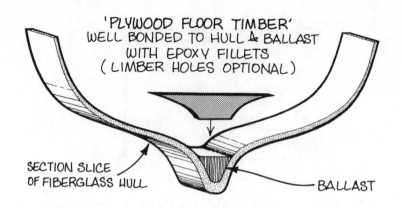

'PLYWOOD FLOOR TIMBER'
WELL BONDED TO HULL & BALLAST
WITH EPOXY FILLETS
(LIMBER HOLES OPTIONAL)

SECTION SLICE
OF FIBERGLASS HULL

BALLAST

increase the hull thickness will help, but the real long-term solution is a bridge, or gusset, spanning the bilge area and connecting the port and starboard sides of the hull, thereby spreading the load throughout the hull rather than concentrating it in a small area. Such gussets also divide up the sometimes considerable bilge storage space into manageable compartments, allowing for much better organization. When the edges are well sheathed with epoxy fillets, the gussets become structural—true floor timbers in the traditional sense.

There are no hard-and-fast rules for the spacing of gussets. One every 16 to 18 inches is a good rule of thumb, but the rule can be easily adjusted around storage needs—for example, to accommodate a marine battery or a water storage tank between gussets.

To install gussets you will usually have to start by removing the cabin sole (but not always—on certain occasions I have been able to gain adequate access through the bilge inspection plates). Removing the sole can turn out to be an advantage, because you can use the old sole to pattern a new one, with hinged or flush-fitting hatches to the storage compartments the gussets will provide. (For more information on how to construct these, see ahead, under "Hatches and Compartments.")

Once you've established clear access, mark the intended location of each gusset and make a cardboard pattern at each location.* Fit the gusset all the way down to the keelson and firmly against the sides of the hull—the wider the span, the better—up to the bottom of the cabin sole. Don't worry about achieving a precision fit; the epoxy fillets will provide the structural bonding and strength. But be sure that the bilge is clean and dry before forming the fillets (this may be the hardest part of the job); trying to bond epoxy to a wet, dirty surface is a waste of time.

---

* Even if you've removed the sole, there should be support cleats or marks remaining on the hull to identify its location.

Transom Reinforcements

The transom is another area that may benefit from additional support. On traditional wooden boats you will always find fashion pieces, molded reinforcing strips around the perimeter of the transom to provide extra fastening surface for the important hull-to-transom connection, but many glass hulls have no additional reinforcement here—only the normal number of hull laminations. Since the transom often holds the rudder, outboard motor, and other hefty gear, additional reinforcements are well worth the time and effort.

A large-diameter epoxy fillet applied to the inside corners of the transom is a simple and effective means of gaining additional support for a glass hull, and the mailing tube ribs described earlier are a another method well suited to the inside of a transom. A more complicated solution is to partition off the sterndeck area with structural fore-and-aft bulkheads, which give additional bracing to the transom while providing lazarette storage as well. (The construction of full and partial bulkheads will be discussed ahead, on pages 59–65.) Some weakened or older hulls may also benefit from fiberglass tape applied to the outside edges of the transom to reinforce this critical joint that often takes a lot of abuse. Wash the gelcoat to remove wax; scrape or sand lightly to remove paint; then apply the tape, using epoxy resin to saturate. Once the epoxy has kicked, the edges can be faired with a wide putty knife and thickened epoxy; then the whole works can be painted over.

Deck Reinforcements

Curved shape is a valuable tool of the fiberglass boat designer because it adds strength without appreciable weight. Decks of small glass boats are a potentially vulnerable area since many of them have virtually no crown at all, making them far weaker than a section of laminate with pronounced camber. Walking on a single layer glass deck, one unsupported by a foam sandwich, balsa, or honeycomb core, can produce a motion similar to the oil canning action of a weak hull. Bulkheads intended to give support may be entirely inadequate for the job, or spaced too far apart.

The final solution for most problems that ail a glass deck is to rip it right off the hull and replace it with a plywood deck, but this is a major retrofit and probably best saved for a last resort. Among the numerous less drastic options for reinforcing a spongy deck are additional fiberglass laminations, wood deck overlays, exterior and interior deck beams, full and partial bulkheads, and samson posts.

Exterior Deck and Cabin Beams

Exterior reinforcements in the form of beams, rails, and moldings have wide applicability on small boats. There are numerous options, ranging from small toerails laid across the deck to substantial "girder" beams to beef up a critical area such as the mast support location. Exterior reinforcements can also come in the form of traditional grabrails, which provide support, improved safety, and a useful place for tying off gear.

The main advantage of exterior (rather than interior) beams for small boats is that they do not take up valuable headroom in the cabin. While providing reinforcement for the deck and cabin top, they allow

The radically crowned deck on this 29-footer adds strength without appreciable weight. Further structural reinforcement is provided by the long fore-and-aft grabrails, which are in fact exterior beams.

a smooth surface on the underside, which means a cleaner look and less head banging. Above decks, they provide good footing and are particularly useful to help you locate yourself at night.

Exterior beams, even substantial ones, need not add excessive weight. Plywood beams offer an outstanding strength-to-weight ratio and can be made to conform to just about any shape. Another option is to build girder-type beams—solid at the top and bottom, with carefully spaced cutouts in the middle—which are as stiff or stiffer than conventional solid beams and can weigh less than half as much. Lamination makes them even stiffer (see ahead). When designing such a beam, consider the potential usefulness of these cutouts as tie-off holes or suitable handholds, and make them large enough to accommodate a gloved hand.

Exterior beams may be located fore and aft, athwartships, or diagonally. Fore and aft beams are more traditional and often used for stowing oars and boathooks on deck. They can also be useful for routing jibsheets to the cockpit or rainwater for catchment. Rigged with lengths of shock cord and tiedowns, they are very handy to hold the odd and assorted pieces of gear necessary on small boats.

Athwartships exterior beams look slightly more radical and are not as aerodynamic as fore and aft beams, although when properly

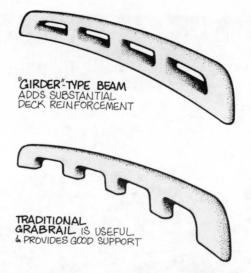

"GIRDER"-TYPE BEAM ADDS SUBSTANTIAL DECK REINFORCEMENT

TRADITIONAL GRABRAIL IS USEFUL & PROVIDES GOOD SUPPORT

designed they look appropriate on most modern hulls. They are sometimes easier to build than other types and probably provide slightly better reinforcement to the deck and cabin top because they span the entire width, tying the sides together.

It is often possible to design exterior reinforcements so that they accomplish several jobs at once. On one of our boats we built a set of girder beams laid athwartships on the cabin top, with the cutouts specifically positioned to accommodate two large sculling oars and a long boathook. The beams also served as a cradle for a dinghy, which was carried upside down on top of the cabin, right over a ventilation hatch. In this way the dinghy provided ventilation for the open hatch and also protected the varnished oars from sunlight and weather.

Plywood Beams

Fashioning beams, planks, and moldings to the complex curves of a boat has always been the essence of the boatbuilder's art. Tradition-

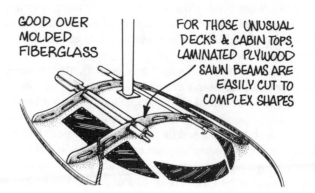

GOOD OVER MOLDED FIBERGLASS

FOR THOSE UNUSUAL DECKS & CABIN TOPS, LAMINATED PLYWOOD SAWN BEAMS ARE EASILY CUT TO COMPLEX SHAPES

ally, beams were either steam bent or else sawn to the shape of the curve; either way was a lot of work. While building forms for making a curved deck, we discovered a far easier solution: to make beams out of plywood, glued up with epoxy in thin vertical laminations. Though untraditional, the beams have surprising strength and stiffness, at far less weight than their solid timber counterparts. This method of construction has two other significant advantages. First, complex shapes can be accomplished easily, in many cases without the need of bending or the use of a laminating form. Second, by using this method you can make your beams almost entirely out of scrap materials, saving your best full-length pieces for the outside layer and using smaller, butt-jointed pieces for the inside layers. Laminations can be glued up either horizontally or vertically, but solid timber is normally used for horizontal or "flat" laminations. The advantages of vertically laminated "sawn" beams are best realized by using plywood.

If you have a constantly cambered shape along a deck or cabin top and a number of beams are needed, it may be worthwhile to build a form and laminate horizontally. Laminating forms are not difficult to build; they can be as simple as the bracket form shown in the accompanying illustration, which is easily adjusted for various shapes. Be sure to use a sheet of plastic over the form to keep the beams from sticking.

If you are making only one or two beams, it may be easier to glue them up right in place, using the shape of the deck or cabin top as the form for the curve. (If you will later attach the beams to the boat by through-bolting, you can predrill the holes and use the bolts for clamping pressure while laminating.) Vertically laminated beams are the easiest to build up on location and do not require a laminating form. We usually cut a pattern to shape, scribe it right to the deck or cabintop location, glue on as many thicknesses as are needed for width, and then remove it for finishing before returning it for final

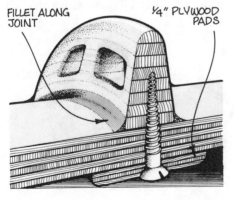

SECTION THROUGH ¾" DECK AND 2" HIGH LAMINATED GIRDER-TYPE BEAM

FILLET ALONG JOINT

¼" PLYWOOD PADS

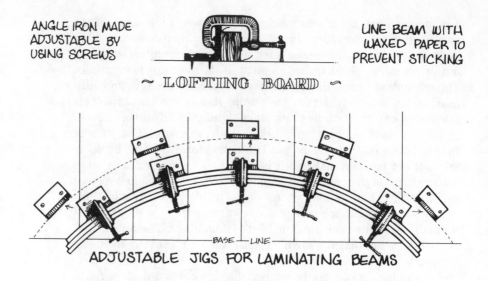

ANGLE IRON MADE
ADJUSTABLE BY
USING SCREWS

LINE BEAM WITH
WAXED PAPER TO
PREVENT STICKING

~ LOFTING BOARD ~

BASE LINE

ADJUSTABLE JIGS FOR LAMINATING BEAMS

attachment. Again, be sure to use a sheet of plastic over the boat to keep the beam from sticking.

Finishing. Finishing "on the bench" is always faster and produces superior work. For one thing, it allows you to glue up slightly over-size, so that you can shave off the glue drips, fine tune the shape, and still end up with the proper size. If the beams must be constructed start to finish on location, great care will need to be taken at each step of the way to ensure that the cuts are accurate and the glue lines tidy.

Take care when cleaning up the beams; handplaning plywood is likely to lift the grain (particularly if you are working with end grain laminations), and epoxy drips are hard on hand tools. Belt sanding will do the trick but also raises a considerable amount of dust. In most cases, the best option is to cut away the excess, using a band saw or jigsaw. The top edges should be rounded with a router (with a 1/2-inch-radius or larger bit) to make them safer on deck if someone should fall on them. At this point, too, you would make any cutouts in the beams, using a drill and jigsaw with a sharp blade. The edges

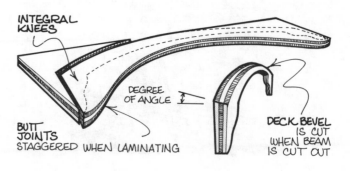

INTEGRAL
KNEES

DEGREE
OF ANGLE

BUTT
JOINTS
STAGGERED WHEN LAMINATING

DECK BEVEL
IS CUT
WHEN BEAM
IS CUT OUT

of the cutouts should also be rounded with a router bit or a wood rasp.

Beams can be tapered from top to bottom to save weight and for a clean, less bulky look. High-quality plywood looks good when laminated, but if the disparity of the wood grain bothers you, the beams can be painted.

Fastening. If you wish the beams to be removable (for a variety of good reasons), they can be bedded and bolted in place. Carriage bolts work well, with the heads placed in countersunk holes, which are sealed with wood plugs.*

A more permanent fastening option for smaller beams is to epoxy glue them in place. On a deck without much shape, the epoxy alone will usually suffice, but for deeper curves you might want to use fastenings to clamp the beams firmly in place during the gluing operation, especially if you're using bent, horizontal laminations. After the epoxy has kicked, the fastenings can be removed.

Be sure to clean the surface well before gluing. Gelcoat should be scraped or sanded; for a critical application, take it right down to the laminate. Once the beam is aligned and the bolt holes predrilled, both surfaces are given a thin coating of catalyzed resin. Then a thickened mixture of epoxy is applied to one of the mating surfaces to fill any unfairness and provide a very strong and reliable bond. On all permanent installations we finish up with an epoxy fillet along each edge. This not only seals the edges of the beams but creates a much stronger bond between the deck and cabintop and increases the bearing area of the beam. These fillets look quite good after they are painted—and the beams seem to grow right out of the boat.

Wood Deck Overlays

Wood deck overlays are among the most aesthetically pleasing ways of providing reinforcement for a weak deck. Traditionally nautical in feeling, they are a popular design feature on many of today's better production and custom boats—and are customarily fastened over fiberglass or plywood.

There are two means of achieving a wood deck. The more traditional is to actually *lay* the deck, using thin (⅝-inch) teak strips (called "strakes") with a caulking seam between each strake. The usual procedure is to lay down bedding compound, position the strake, then fasten from above using a stainless steel self-tapping screw. The screws hold very well in fiberglass, but must be predrilled

---

* Removing the plug for access to the bolt head or nut will probably destroy it, but it may be necessary. When the time comes for removal, drill a small pilot hole through the center of the plug; then insert a wood screw into the hole and tighten. The screw will enter the plug and bottom out on the head of the bolt; as you continue to tighten, it will lift the plug (or pieces of the plug) right out of the hole.

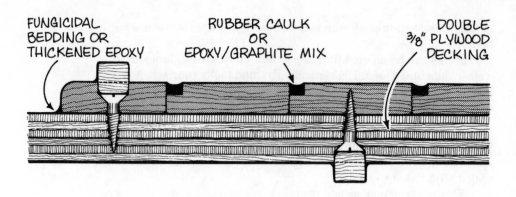

FUNGICIDAL BEDDING OR THICKENED EPOXY

RUBBER CAULK OR EPOXY/GRAPHITE MIX

DOUBLE 3/8" PLYWOOD DECKING

to the proper depth and applied carefully to avoid stripping. After the deck is installed and all fastening holes are countersunk and plugged, deck caulking is normally applied. Good caulking will maintain a watertight bond and will adjust to expansion or contraction of the deck by bulging or shrinking slightly above or below the decking surface.

Traditional teak decking is somewhat thick and is usually suitable only for near-flat areas of the deck or cabintop. An alternative approach is to create an "instant" laid deck out of sheets of veneer glued down with epoxy. Veneer overlays are thin enough to apply over curved areas of the deck and cabintop and are well suited for single-layer fiberglass decks, for which they provide substantial support plus the handsome look of a wood surface. Teak veneer can be oiled, varnished, or left to weather naturally—in which case, it provides an additional degree of non-skid to the surface. If extra strength is needed, additional layers of veneer can be built up over the first. Traditional laid deck caulking grooves are sometimes simulated by using graphite-blackened epoxy, or caulking can be applied between the strips of veneer.

Veneer is easily applied to clean, sanded decks using thickened epoxy. Staples or self-tapping screws with washers will help hold the wood in place until the epoxy kicks, at which time the fastenings are removed. Small lead weights are also useful for holding down narrow strips.

Deck-Stepped Mast Support

On all conventionally rigged sailboats the press of the wind against the sails is converted by the rigging to downward force on the mast and mast step area. If the mast is stepped on the keel, the strain is transferred directly onto the strongest single place in the hull, but deck-stepped masts rely on interior bulkheads and decks to absorb the strain of sailing. The mast step area often needs stiffening, particularly on racers with a lot of campaigns under their keels and on older boats that have upgraded their rigging, placing increased stress on the support structure. Often on a beam reach or when straining to windward you can see the bulkhead under the mast support flexing slightly and the deck compressing under the load of a deck-stepped mast. Sometimes the lee rigging will go slack as the mast forces itself farther down into the deck.

Strengthening the mast support area in small fiberglass hulls is usually a two-part operation. The first step is to add a mast support pad to increase the bearing area of the mast step on the deck, spreading the downward pressure over a larger area. The second part involves beefing up bulkheads and underdeck supports.

Mast Support Pad

A mast support pad can be fashioned out of any number of materials. For those who enjoy working with metal, an aluminum, stainless steel, or bronze plate will serve the purpose nicely. An all-fiberglass pad is another option, but our own choice is epoxy-laminated plywood. A large, stiff plywood pad works well on deck because quality plywood has excellent compression while weighing only about half as much as glass laminate of the same dimensions. Epoxy is used to laminate and glue the pad in place.

The dimensions of the pad, and its method of construction, will vary with the size of the boat and the amount of deck curvature in the mast support area. Eighteen inches by 24 inches, with a thickness of ⅜ inch to ⅝ inch, is about average for a boat in the 20 to 25 foot range. If the deck surface is extremely flat, you might be able to achieve this with a single piece of plywood, but normally you will have to form the pad as if building a cold-molded hull, using narrow strips of plywood (4 inches is typical) to achieve the linear dimensions, and two or more laminations to reach the desired thickness. If the deck has substantial curvature in the mast support area, ⅛-inch-thick veneer can be substituted for plywood.

The first job is to remove the mast step plate, which may turn out to be either through-bolted, screwed, or riveted in position. Once the area is clear and clean, the instructions are essentially the same as for a wood deck overlay. Begin by sanding and scraping away most of the gelcoat to obtain a good gluing surface; then lay the wood strips. Short staples or self-tapping screws with washers can be used to hold the strips temporarily in place until the epoxy kicks, or lead

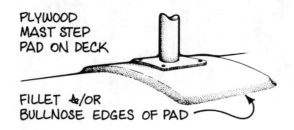

PLYWOOD MAST STEP PAD ON DECK

FILLET &/OR BULLNOSE EDGES OF PAD

½" - ¾" THICK
PLYWOOD
FASTENED WITH
PHILLIPS SCREWS

PLYWOOD COLLAR FOR
MAST SUPPORT POST

weights may be sufficient. Once completed, the pad may be sheathed in glass if you prefer, and the edges should be tapered or beveled for safety on deck and a more finished look. Any access holes for the mast wiring or the mast step plate hardware should be drilled slightly oversize, and the edges of the holes should be well sealed with epoxy to prevent possible watersoak damage to the plywood. The rigging, when replaced, must be slacked according to the thickness of the pad.

Interior Mast Support

The other part of proper mast support lies beneath the deck, with an appropriately located post or bulkhead. If there is no room below for a full or partial bulkhead, a single post (or "strongback") located directly under the mast and placed firmly on the ballast casting or a floor timber—not merely on the hull liner—will usually suffice. The post can be epoxy laminated out of smaller pieces of timber for greater strength, much like the plywood beams already discussed. A plywood collar at top and bottom will hold the post exactly in position, and

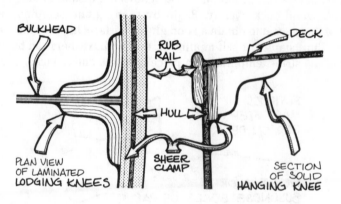

BULKHEAD

DECK

RUB
RAIL

HULL

PLAN VIEW
OF LAMINATED
LODGING KNEES

SHEER
CLAMP

SECTION
OF SOLID
HANGING KNEE

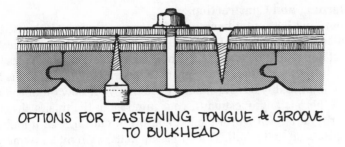

OPTIONS FOR FASTENING TONGUE & GROOVE
TO BULKHEAD

removing or replacing the post becomes a simple matter of removing a few screws from the collar.

Weak bulkheads can be stiffened in a variety of ways. The most radical solution is to remove and replace the entire bulkhead with a new, stiffer structure (to be discussed in detail in the next section). Short of removal, weak bulkheads can be strengthened by adding on timber or plywood doublers, by installing knees on either side, or by the simple and aesthetically pleasing treatment of tongue-and-groove timber paneling screwed and glued onto the bulkhead. Softwood tongue and groove, such as spruce, fir, and cedar, brightens the interior and provides a golden glow in the light of an oil lamp; hardwoods such as teak and yacal look even more classic when finished bright. One inch by four inches is a good width for tongue and groove for small boats.

To install tongue-and-groove paneling, start the first (or master) strake on the center, or at the edge of the hatch cutout, and make sure it is vertical since it will be the guide for all the others on either side. Drill the screw holes; then remove the strake and vacuum up the dust. Apply glue to both sides and replace the strake. The screw holes are usually sealed with matching plugs. You may wish to finish around the hatch cutout with a plastic molding or a sectioned wood molding.

Bulkheads

Few single operations can increase the strength of a small hull as much as adding a bulkhead. Bulkheads tie the hull sides together, reinforce and support the deck, act as floor timbers and ribs, and can function as watertight divisions and organizers below decks or in the cockpit.

If the saving of weight is vitally important, a hollow ultralight bulkhead can be constructed of two faces of $\frac{1}{8}$-inch hardwood plywood, with spruce spacers between the plywood to provide added stiffness. Not only are such bulkheads very light and quite stiff, but they also can provide insulation and positive flotation if fitted out with blocks of foam between the spaces. Epoxy is used to seal each chamber, making the whole structure watertight.

Patterning and Construction

If your boat has a hull liner, your first major choice will be whether to attach the new bulkhead to the liner or to cut through the liner and attach it directly to the hull. There are no hard and fast rules here. If the liner is structural and appears to be firmly attached to the hull, you will probably be safe enough attaching your new bulkhead to it. But if there is any question in your mind as to the liner's structural integrity, it is well worth the extra effort to cut through it and affix the bulkhead to the hull. You will sleep better at night knowing your bulkhead is firmly attached to something structural, not just swimming around inside the hull. A typical bulkhead-to-hull installation is shown in top view in the accompanying illustration.

When patterning full or partial bulkheads for very small hulls the easiest method is simply to start with a large sheet of cardboard and trim it with a pair of scissors until it fits. If you can easily determine the centerline for the hull, you can also pattern half the bulkhead and then flip the cardboard over to draw the remaining half, but a true centerline is required for this method.

For larger hulls there are better ways to pattern bulkheads. Anything over four feet wide is best patterned using the standard shipwright's batten, or bulkhead patterning stick. This is especially true for round-bottomed hulls with pronounced tumblehome (convex curve as the hull sides approach the sheer line), because unlike hard chine and simpler hulls, the bulkhead cannot be fitted into these hulls in successive steps, trimming as needed until the plywood fits. The bulkhead patterning stick is a time and materials saver.

A patterning stick can be very simple, a piece of scrap plywood, or it can be quite fancy and individual, made from finest teak or rosewood. Either way, it should be thin (about ¼ inch is average) and slightly longer than half the beam of your boat. On one end is a sharp pointer, and one side (or both sides) has a series of notches or

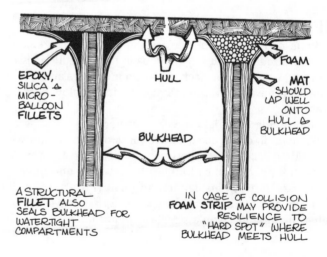

EPOXY, SILICA & MICRO-BALLOON FILLETS

HULL

FOAM

MAT SHOULD LAP WELL ONTO HULL & BULKHEAD

BULKHEAD

A STRUCTURAL FILLET ALSO SEALS BULKHEAD FOR WATERTIGHT COMPARTMENTS

IN CASE OF COLLISION FOAM STRIP MAY PROVIDE RESILIENCE TO "HARD SPOT" WHERE BULKHEAD MEETS HULL

teeth, like a giant handsaw. There are identifying numbers at intervals along the notches (see illustration).

Use is very simple. A cardboard or scrap plywood pattern board of any convenient size is clamped in place exactly on the plane of the planned bulkhead. Holding the patterning stick flat against the pattern board, you then extend the pointer out to touch the hull at various locations. Use a sharp pencil to trace a series of sections of the stick onto the pattern board, copying the indentation or tooth number onto each tracing so it will be easy to duplicate the position of the stick later. If there is extreme curvature to the hull, make the tracing locations close together, but if the hull is relatively straight-sided, the reference points can be farther apart. Work your way all around the perimeter of the bulkhead, making overlapping tracings until you have enough reference points to duplicate the shape of the bulkhead. Then take the pattern board out of the hull, lay it on the sheet of plywood to be used for the bulkhead, and again place the stick on each of the tracing locations. From there on it's just a game of "connect-the-dots" to duplicate the shape of the bulkhead. For bulkheads intended for the forepeak area, you may also wish to mark and cut the appropriate bevel on the edge of the bulkhead.

Used with care, the patterning stick will provide a close fit, which can be trimmed slightly for a perfect fit. Bulkheads for fiberglass and cold-molded hulls should be drawn and cut slightly undersize to allow room for thickened epoxy to squeeze around and behind the bulkhead to seal the plywood edge grain. Bulkheads for plank-on-frame hulls need to be as accurate as possible; otherwise it will be necessary to spend substantial time applying a molding to the joint where the bulkhead meets the hull and deck. Epoxy fillets are usually

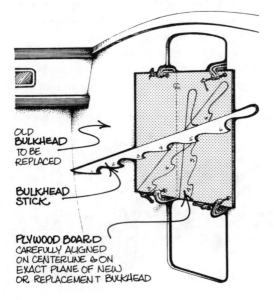

OLD BULKHEAD TO BE REPLACED

BULKHEAD STICK

PLYWOOD BOARD CAREFULLY ALIGNED ON CENTERLINE & ON EXACT PLANE OF NEW OR REPLACEMENT BULKHEAD

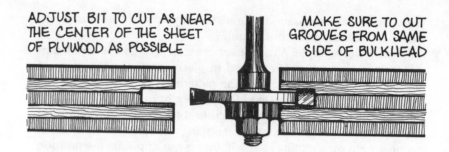

ADJUST BIT TO CUT AS NEAR THE CENTER OF THE SHEET OF PLYWOOD AS POSSIBLE

MAKE SURE TO CUT GROOVES FROM SAME SIDE OF BULKHEAD

not recommended for plank-on-frame hulls because of the moisture sometimes present in the wood.

Large bulkheads, wider than one sheet of plywood, should be made in halves and joined at the centerline, using a spline joint held together with epoxy glue (see illustration). To make a proper spline joint, you'll need a router and a sharp splining bit. (Make sure it's sharp; a dull one is dangerous.) A carbide roller bearing bit is vastly superior to a steel bit and will last many times longer, while cutting clean, deep spline holes. The bits we use cut a $\frac{9}{16}$-inch-deep spline groove into each half of the bulkhead, which means that a one-inch-wide spline will fit easily and still allow for glue in the joint. For most medium and large bulkheads a bit that cuts a $\frac{1}{4}$-inch-wide groove is sufficient, and with care it may be used on bulkheads as thin as $\frac{3}{8}$ inch. Bulkheads thinner than that require a $\frac{1}{8}$-inch splining bit. Cut the splines themselves from quality plywood, so that the opposing laminations of veneer will provide the support for the flush joint.

Adjust the bit to cut as near as possible to the center of a sheet of plywood, and make it a point to cut both halves of the bulkhead from the same side of the plywood. This is a necessary precaution because the bit is seldom really in the exact center of the plywood edge. Being slightly off center is no problem so long as the two mating pieces are off center by the same amount.

When making a two-part bulkhead some builders fit it into the hull a half at a time, but we prefer whenever possible to join the halves on the bench and insert them into the boat in one piece, because it affords better control during the glue-up. Slather the spline and both sides of the groove with epoxy, and tap the spline carefully into place

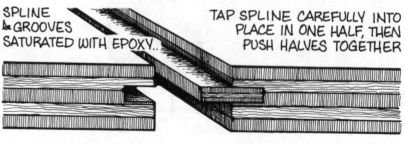

SPLINE & GROOVES SATURATED WITH EPOXY..

TAP SPLINE CAREFULLY INTO PLACE IN ONE HALF, THEN PUSH HALVES TOGETHER

A carbide-tipped splining or slotting bit (above), showing an extra "wing," or cutter. The bit disassembles by removing the nut and guide bearing, and the cutter can be replaced with another of a different size.

in one half; then push the other half of the bulkhead into place. If for some reason the two pieces won't mate properly, screw a couple of billy blocks onto the face of the plywood and attach a sliding clamp to apply more pressure. If the bulkhead bends from the clamping pressure, clamp a straightedge on the other side to keep it flat, or else it will take a permanent warp. When the glue kicks, remove any clamps and sand the joint flush; it is now ready for installation in the hull. If there are bevels, they should be rough cut with a jigsaw set at the correct angle, then cleaned up and fine tuned with block plane and bevel measure. If the large bulkhead is flimsy, it may need a temporary brace clamped or screwed across the halves.

Fitting

When fitting stiff bulkheads into small hulls—particularly thin fiberglass hulls—take care not to force, in the process damaging or changing the shape of the hull. If there are previously installed bulkheads or furniture, it's all too easy to tear something loose by wedging in a bulkhead that is slightly too large. It's best to make a loose fit, striving for a gap of approximately ¼ inch all around the perimeter— just right for applying an epoxy fillet. Caution is particularly urged if you are trimming out a new bare hull. Empty glass hulls can be quite floppy, and forcing an oversize or incorrectly shaped bulkhead is likely to alter the hull shape. It's a good idea to check bulkhead patterns against the original lofting lines if at all possible.

To ensure that the bulkhead is aligned athwartships in the hull, it's wise to take a series of measurements from various places. If there

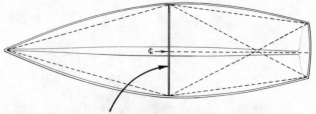

TO ENSURE THAT A NEW **BULKHEAD** IS **ALIGNED ATHWARTSHIPS** IN THE HULL, TAKE A SERIES OF MEASUREMENTS AS SHOWN ABOVE

are other bulkheads in the hull, they can be used for reference, but when installing new bulkheads we usually measure from each corner of the transom to the place where the bulkhead meets the hull. Once these measurements are obtained, we measure from a given centerline point at the bow to both sides of the bulkhead.

If you're certain the hull is sitting level fore and aft, you can install the bulkhead plumb by using a framing square and level. But there is no absolute dictum that says all bulkheads must be perfectly plumb; after all, this is a boat, not a condominium. The after end of the cabin bulkhead is sometimes best installed at an angle, to provide a more comfortable backrest when relaxing in the cockpit. In the forepeak, you might want to consider using a cant bulkhead, which is installed not vertically but at an angle—generally a right angle—to the stem. This angle also provides the best support and resistance in the event of a collision.

Finishing

We usually finish nicely grained hardwood plywood by sanding and applying a few coats of varnish, but a light-colored paint is sometimes an easier and more functional option for a small, crowded hull. If a bulkhead needs additional stiffness, tongue-and-groove timber can be applied to the face, following the instructions given in the preceding section. An epoxy fillet is used to trim out the perimeter.

Any passageway openings in the bulkhead need some sort of moldings around the perimeter. Traditional bulkhead openings are framed with a pieced teak molding, carefully and tediously fitted. This is a nice treatment if it can be accomplished with a professional touch, but amateurish work, with large gaps and disparate grain, looks very bad. An alternative treatment that often saves considerably on labor and materials is to wrap veneer around the perimeter of the bulkhead opening. A piece of ⅛-inch veneer will bend to a radius of approximately 18 inches, and thinner veneer will bend even more tightly for sharper curves and smaller shapes. (This same treatment works for table edging and other cabinetry and is a good way to use up leftover scraps of veneer.)

If the cutout is oval or round, try to lay the veneer on in one

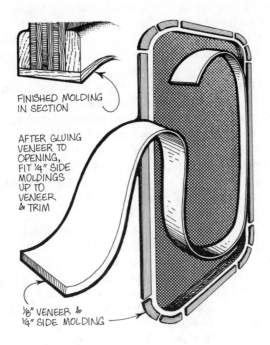

FINISHED MOLDING
IN SECTION

AFTER GLUING
VENEER TO
OPENING,
FIT ¼" SIDE
MOLDINGS
UP TO
VENEER
& TRIM

⅛" VENEER &
¼" SIDE MOLDING

continuous piece, with only one seam in the least conspicuous place, either under a footpad or overhead. Position it with temporary staples, and glue the veneer in place using thickened epoxy. Be sure to leave enough of an overhang on each face of the plywood to attach a side molding if necessary. After the epoxy kicks, pull the staples and apply your choice of side moldings, or carefully block plane the veneer flush with the plywood. Another option is to apply three or more layers of veneer over the first. Then, when the epoxy kicks, simply round the edges and the molding is finished. If the bottom of the cutout is used as a step, it can be protected with a piece of leather held in place with brass tacks.

Samson Post

A samson post or towing bitt, properly designed and installed, has any number of uses aboard a boat. It can reinforce the deck and provide major structural support to what otherwise might be a flimsy area. At the same time, it provides a well-supported attachment point for securing anchor lines and tow lines. On some small boats it can even be used for winching.

Design and Construction

A post need not be very tall to work effectively; in fact, very short posts are usually stronger, safer, and less apt to get in the way on deck. The only reason to make a post tall is if it's used all the time and needs to be placed at a convenient working height—as, for example, an after towing or hoisting bitt on a workboat.

Posts and bitts are traditionally oak or hardwood, but even softwoods like fir and tamarack make strong yet lightweight posts when sealed with epoxy. Large posts usually should be laminated, rather than shaped from a single piece of wood, for strength and to prevent warping and cracking over time. For instance, two 2 × 4s laminated together will make a post 3 inches square that will be stronger—and less expensive—than a 3-inch-square timber. When laminating it is best to use epoxy glue because of its superior bonding strength. In these larger posts, a slight taper is important to provide flexibility and a measure of shock absorbency to prevent the post from breaking under sudden strain. Smaller posts need little or no taper.

When shaping it is a good idea to round all sharp corners on the post, both above and below decks. This makes it easier on lines— and also on your head if you should bang the post while rummaging in the forepeak. Rounded corners are attractive in their own right and also help the finish last longer because a sharp corner gets dinged much more easily than a blunt, rounded corner. A wood rasp and block plane will sculpture the corner bevels and provide a pleasing shape. If additional padding is necessary, the post can be wrapped in leather or some other shock-absorbing material.

The post should be sealed with three coats of epoxy; afterwards it can be painted or finished bright. A sealed, painted post is maintenance-free for years, but a bright finish over the epoxy will require yearly maintenance to keep it looking good. The end grain on top the post also needs protection; the traditional method is to use sheet lead or brass, which can be gently hammered to a perfect fit, then tacked in place with bronze or brass tacks.

Many owners prefer to stick a pin horizontally through the top of the post to form a cleat shape as an aid in tying off and securing lines. Old bronze keel bolts work very well on larger posts. To insert them permanently, drill a slightly oversize hole, clean and file the pin

CUTAWAY ON DECK NEAR CENTERLINE SHOWING TAPERED POST

PLYWOOD DOUBLERS & CLEATS BELOW DECK

POST BOLTED TO FRAME, SOLE OR FLOOR TIMBER

TOW OR ANCHOR LINE LED THROUGH "CAPTIVE" BOW ROLLER

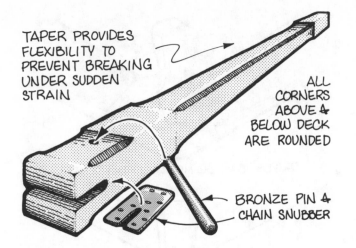

TAPER PROVIDES
FLEXIBILITY TO
PREVENT BREAKING
UNDER SUDDEN
STRAIN

ALL
CORNERS
ABOVE &
BELOW DECK
ARE ROUNDED

BRONZE PIN &
CHAIN SNUBBER

to rough up its surface, and glue it in place with thickened epoxy. Round the corners of the pin to prevent barking your shins.

Ideally, the post should be located out of high traffic areas but easily accessible to whatever operations it is being used for. It does not necessarily have to be on the centerline of the boat. But keep in mind that towing lines and sea anchors, in particular, need to be led from as close to the centerline as possible; if you locate the post off center, you will want to arrange fairleads or even cleats to route a line directly forward or aft on centerline. Try to position the post so that there is minimal interference with the sail control lines.

When planning installation of a post, you also need to make provision for protecting the caprails from abrasion caused by dragging lines or chain over them. This may require metal rubbing strips, sacrificial wood strips, perhaps a hawsepipe under the caprail, or even possibly a bow or stern roller (see sidebar).

Attachment and Bracing
The methods of attachment and bracing are important, and they differ for every boat. The post must be able to cope with a sudden shock

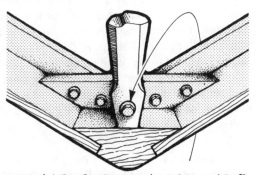

POST CAN BE BOLTED TO A FLOOR TIMBER

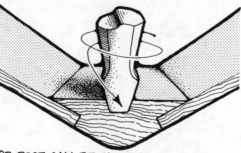

OR POST CAN BE NOTCHED INTO KEEL

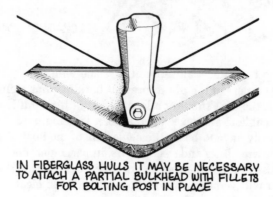

IN FIBERGLASS HULLS IT MAY BE NECESSARY
TO ATTACH A PARTIAL BULKHEAD WITH FILLETS
FOR BOLTING POST IN PLACE

from any direction, fore and aft or athwartships, and should be braced accordingly. It should be attached at the bottom by bolting to a structural member or by bolting and mortising into a floor timber. It can be attached to a forepeak sole, but in order for the attachment to be structural, the sole must be well braced. A bulkhead is an ideal attachment point since it provides support at both top and bottom while still allowing a degree of flexibility in case of a sudden, extremely hard pull. An anchor locker bulkhead makes a good attachment point for a samson post; lazarette bulkheads are fine for quarter bitts (stern towing bitts).

In fiberglass hulls without obvious bracing options it may be necessary to build a partial bulkhead, gusset, or brace as a support member for the post. Such bulkheads and bracings can be attached directly to the hull with epoxy fillets, provided the surface has been properly prepared.* Alternatively, a plywood gusset fillet across the forepeak, much like a floor timber, will hold the bottom of the post in place and also reinforce the hull. (Construction of gussets has been discussed earlier, on pages 47-48.) Once the gusset is in place, the post can be bolted or screwed to it.

---

* For glass hulls this means clean, sanded, and dry. Aluminum hulls also need sanding and possibly an etching treatment, which can be recommended and supplied by your epoxy dealer.

For bracing at deck level, where the most strain will occur, the post ideally should be bolted to a deck beam, but if your boat doesn't have deck beams, or if the spacing is inconvenient, then deck doublers of plywood are a satisfactory solution. The doublers should extend over as large an area as is feasible, from one beam to another, or to the next bulkhead, or from sheer clamp to sheer clamp. They are usually placed below the deck but can also be above it if they don't interfere with traffic and you don't object to the look.

Plywood makes superior doublers because of its resistance to splitting. It will also bend slightly to conform to deck camber, and if the camber is extreme you can use a number of thin laminations instead of one thicker, stiffer piece. For most boats under 30 feet, ½-inch-thick plywood (whether a single piece or multiple laminations) will provide sufficient strength.

Doublers should be fastened permanently in place using screws and slightly thickened epoxy. For additional clamping pressure during the glue-up, you might want to cut the hole for the post at this point in the operation to enable the use of C-clamps around its perimeter. You can also rig additional shoring from below.

The post and deck doublers are reinforced by timber cleats (small, supportive pieces of wood) screwed or glued into the post. These cleats are primary support members for the deck and also help to make the flexible seam watertight. They should run continuously around the perimeter of the post under the doublers and the deck. On a small boat, they would normally be ¾ inch thick by ¾ inch wide.

When cutting the deck hole for the post, make it slightly oversize—as much as ⅛ inch all around the perimeter—to allow for sealing the edge grain of the cut with epoxy. As a further safeguard against eventual rot or leaks, form a finger-sized fillet of either epoxy/microballoons or caulking around the post where it meets the deck. If the post is to be installed permanently, an epoxy/microballoon mixture is a good bedding choice that is very strong while still retaining

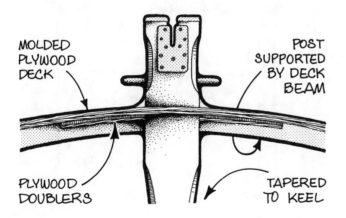

MOLDED
PLYWOOD
DECK

POST
SUPPORTED
BY DECK
BEAM

PLYWOOD
DOUBLERS

TAPERED
TO KEEL

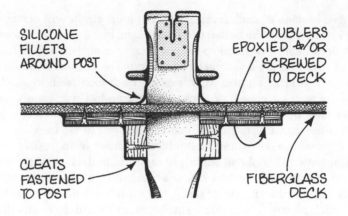

SILICONE FILLETS AROUND POST

DOUBLERS EPOXIED &/OR SCREWED TO DECK

CLEATS FASTENED TO POST

FIBERGLASS DECK

some flexibility. Posts that may need to be removed should have a silicone seal or other flexible caulking to ensure watertightness.

The after face of the post is a good location for a chain snubber. A snubber is a bronze or stainless steel plate with a slot to accommodate the anchor chains, and it is a handy device aboard a small boat, especially when you are sailing shorthanded or singlehanded. It can give you a break to catch your breath when raising a heavy anchor, and it will also help to break a stubborn anchor out of rocks

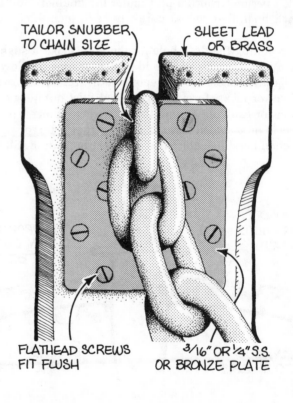

TAILOR SNUBBER TO CHAIN SIZE

SHEET LEAD OR BRASS

FLATHEAD SCREWS FIT FLUSH

3/16" OR 1/4" S.S. OR BRONZE PLATE

Laminated Plywood Bow Rollers

Rollers are quite handy for hoisting an anchor. They reduce strain and friction, protect the sides of the hull, and when used with a winch or chain snubber make breaking out a stubborn anchor much easier. A roller is traditionally placed at the bow, but it can be located aft, over the transom, or on the beam—anywhere it will provide the necessary room and leverage for use.

After looking all over for a bow roller of just the right size and shape for a small boat we were building, we gave up and decided to build a plug (form) so we could have our roller cast in bronze at a foundry. We designed the roller, drew it to scale, and started building the plug with thin discs of hardwood plywood glued together with epoxy. Since we were working without a lathe, we cut each disc to the exact shape and stacked them to match the desired profile. We centerpunched and drilled the center holes on a drill press, then stuck a bolt through all the discs to make clamping easier with the slippery epoxy. After clamping all the discs together with sliding clamps, we carefully removed the center bolt and let the epoxy kick.

Next we smoothed the edges of the plywood discs with a variety of rasps and half round files and sanded until smooth. Then we redrilled the center bolt hole slightly oversize, stopped one end with duct tape, and filled the freshly drilled hole with epoxy mixed with graphite powder. When the mixture hardened and the bolt hole was redrilled to the proper size, the graphite provided enough lubrication to help the roller turn easily under load, and the epoxy had sealed the plywood edge grain to prevent water absorption. After shaping and final sanding, the entire roller was sealed with three coats of epoxy.

And how about the bronze casting for the foundry? Well, our plywood-and-epoxy plug turned out so strong and so well shaped that we forgot all about the foundry and put the plug right on the boat. It works great. And it's the best place we've ever found to stow a CQR anchor on a small boat, chocked securely in place and ready to go in less than a minute.

Since our accidental prototype, we have made several more rollers, with continued success. The plywood rollers are lightweight compared to solid bronze (and much less expensive), somewhat quieter than metal rollers, and easily modified to suit your individual requirements. We've discovered a few design refinements as well. Teflon washers added to the ends will reduce friction when pulling sideways, as is often the case when the roller is being used to break out a single anchor, and a slight amount of silica added to the epoxy mixture used for sealing will produce a slightly harder, more abrasion resistant surface for rolling chain.

The roller can be mounted in the pulpit or on traditional bronze or stainless steel supports. For a small, lightweight boat, it is also possible to fabricate wooden mounts out of hardwood plywood and epoxy, which eliminates almost all metalwork. On boats with bowsprits or stern sprits, the roller can simply be bolted in place—the easiest mounting solution of all.

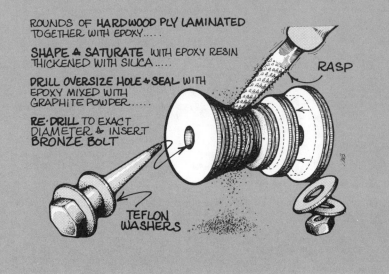

ROUNDS OF HARDWOOD PLY LAMINATED TOGETHER WITH EPOXY.....

SHAPE & SATURATE WITH EPOXY RESIN THICKENED WITH SILICA.....

DRILL OVERSIZE HOLE & SEAL WITH EPOXY MIXED WITH GRAPHITE POWDER.....

RE-DRILL TO EXACT DIAMETER & INSERT BRONZE BOLT

RASP

TEFLON WASHERS

or weed. In fact, the rougher the water, the better the snubber works: You simply take up all the slack you can get, then slide a link of the chain into the snubber slot and relax while the motion of the boat does the work. A bow roller will make this operation even easier by eliminating friction and allowing you to pull straight back instead of lifting the anchor and chain up from the bottom.

Repairing and Reinforcing Rudders and Centerboards

Many rudders are original equipment on older boats, and over the course of time they may warp and rot. One day I looked over the transom of our small sailboat and noticed the rudder's trailing edge had developed a definite curve to starboard. The paint on the solid mahogany blade had cracked and moisture had entered the wood, swelling and splitting it, which explained why we had to pull the tiller to one side even when sailing dead downwind. The rudder had also weakened to the point where its trailing edge could easily be flexed, and around each bolt and screw hole was a black, softened area where salt water had attacked the fastenings, leaching metallic salts into the wood.

These problems are typical of older rudders, and are not confined just to those of solid wood construction. Other common types of rudders, particularly on small glass boats, include fiberglass over wood, solid fiberglass, and fiberglass over a foam core. Corrosion around fastenings, plus the inevitable scrapes and hard knocks that are part of life for a small boat rudder, may eventually penetrate the gelcoat, opening the way to watersoak damage to the laminate. The same hazards hold true—perhaps even more so—for centerboards.

One solution is to build a completely new rudder or centerboard. If the rot is advanced or widespread, or if you are doing a systematic upgrading of the entire boat from stem to stern, rebuilding is probably the best long-range option. In many cases, however, repair is just as effective and far less time-consuming.

Repairing the Damage

Even before you make the decision whether to rebuild or repair, the first step is to remove and inspect the rudder and components. If the

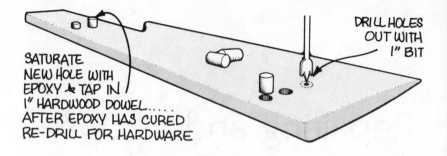

SATURATE
NEW HOLE WITH
EPOXY & TAP IN
1" HARDWOOD DOWEL......
AFTER EPOXY HAS CURED
RE-DRILL FOR HARDWARE

DRILL HOLES
OUT WITH
1" BIT

hardware is in good shape it can be reused, but bolts that are corroded or badly worn should be replaced with new ones made of quality alloys like 316L stainless steel or silicone bronze. Pintles and gudgeons should be inspected as well; if you replace one or the other, make sure the alloys are compatible.

If corroded fastenings have weakened the surrounding wood or fiberglass, it may be necessary to redrill the bolt holes. Follow the procedure described on pages 39-40, or in the accompanying illustration. As soon as you get the hardware removed, dig out all suspect, rotten, or watersoaked wood, foam, or glass, and get a fan blowing on the surface to dry things out. This may take a few days, but no repairs should be started until everything is completely dry. Make a final thorough exploration of the rudder or board with a sharp awl and chisel, to be sure all remaining wood, glass, or foam is healthy. Then you can begin to contemplate repair procedures.

On a solid wood rudder, the usual procedure is to build the rudder back out to its original size using filler pieces, known as Dutchmen, held in place with epoxy. Traditionally this repair method involved quite a bit of fussy, time-consuming work. The damaged area had to be dug out to as symmetrical a shape as possible—preferably square or rectangular—and a new piece of wood, exactly the same dimensions, fitted to close tolerances. Modern epoxy makes the fit somewhat less critical; in fact, if the damaged area is small enough, it's perfectly all right to make the whole repair with epoxy. For wider damage, you'll probably want to go with more traditional Dutchmen

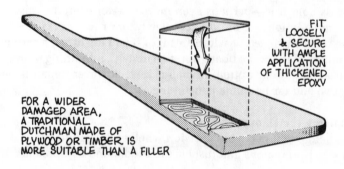

FIT
LOOSELY
& SECURE
WITH AMPLE
APPLICATION
OF THICKENED
EPOXY

FOR A WIDER
DAMAGED AREA,
A TRADITIONAL
DUTCHMAN MADE OF
PLYWOOD OR TIMBER IS
MORE SUITABLE THAN A FILLER

made of plywood or timber, since solid epoxy adds considerable weight.

On a solid glass or glass-and-foam rudder there are various repair options. Plywood or timber can be used, just as on a solid wood rudder, so long as it is well attached and well sealed with epoxy. An alternative approach, particularly useful if the damage is extensive or saving weight is a priority, is to build up the surface using foam sheets or blocks, readily available from various suppliers (you'll see their advertisements in the boating magazines). Rebuilding to the original size is a simple process of attaching the foam and fairing with a thickened mixture of epoxy and microballoons. This mixture is structural, adding considerable strength, yet it can be planed and sanded, and more can be added at any time.

One word of caution: Be sure the epoxy you use is compatible with the foam in your rudder, or the foam you use for building up the surface. Usually this is no problem: if the foam is compatible with polyester, chances are good that it is also compatible with epoxy. The only way to be sure, however, is to do a small test patch. If the epoxy cures without melting the foam, you can assume you have a compatible match.

Depending on the size and shape of your rudder, there is a variety of tools that produce good results. A Surform tool may be helpful in shaping wood, glass, and foam; its blades are available in concave, flat, and convex shapes. A block plane is always helpful, and sometimes a half round rasp will reach into corners where nothing else will work. Final shaping can be completed with sandpaper on a long flexible block.

Reinforcing Critical Areas

Once damaged areas are repaired and the surface is planed and sanded fair, you may want to think about further reinforcements both above and below the waterline. Fiberglass sheathing will add considerable strength and abrasion resistance to underwater areas. Six-ounce fiberglass cloth is a good choice and can be doubled for twice the strength, or you can resort to multiple layers of even heavier cloth, or even glass mat or roving (but remember that mat and roving will have to be filled and faired to produce a smooth, finished looking surface).

Another excellent choice is carbon fiber, which adds strength without appreciable weight. It works equally well on wood and glass, and when properly applied, it is so stiff and strong that it takes nearly all the strain on a rudder or centerboard blade—even the considerable sideloading pressure on a centerboard or daggerboard when at speed. Carbon fiber comes tightly wound on a reel, looking deceptively manageable. Each strand of fibers, known as a tow, comes with a sizing that holds the fibers aligned on a paper backing, but handle them carefully because if they get away they're hard, if not impossible, to recapture.

To apply carbon fiber, start by cutting a grid pattern of shallow grooves in the surface of the rudder blade using a carbide router bit. It's important to make a matching pattern on both sides of the blade to keep everything in balance and strength values consistent. A thin batten tacked in place will function as an edge guide for the router and can be moved and positioned for each pass. When all the grooves are cut, saturate them with epoxy resin, and lay a tow of carbon fiber in each one. Then use a wide putty knife to spread a mixture of epoxy, silica, and microballoons over the grooves. After the epoxy cures, sand the blade surface smooth, then sheath if necessary with glass cloth.

The upper part of the rudder can usually also profit from reinforcement. From just below the tiller head fitting to the waterline, the sides of the rudder are exposed to wrenching forces, which increase in proportion to the area of the rudder blade underwater. A following sea that catches a boat almost stalled at the bottom of a wave trough will place exceptional strain on the rudder and fittings, particularly on a rudder with a long stock from blade to tiller head. When building or rebuilding a rudder, give some thought to methods of making this part of the structure as strong as possible, yet slightly flexible to absorb shock.

The traditional method for stiffening this area is to install cheeks, symmetrically paired doublers (see illustration). Quality hardwood plywood is the material of choice for this job; it is as strong as timber and much more durable for the twisting action common to rudder cheeks and blades. The separate laminations of veneer in plywood are also a considerable visual aid to the shaping process, allowing you to match both sides without actually measuring. The new cheeks should extend from just below the tiller head fitting down almost to the waterline. If there are old cheeks, they can be used for patterning. New plywood cheeks should be glued in place with epoxy rather than fastened with screws or bolts. This eliminates expense, weight, and possible future headaches since metal fastenings are not compatible

UNDERWATER SECTION REINFORCED WITH TOWS OF CARBON FIBER EPOXIED INTO ¾" WIDE GROOVES

HARDWOOD PLYWOOD CHEEKS LAMINATED TO UPPER AREA AND EDGES ARE FILLETED

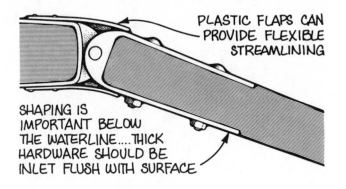

PLASTIC FLAPS CAN PROVIDE FLEXIBLE STREAMLINING

SHAPING IS IMPORTANT BELOW THE WATERLINE....THICK HARDWARE SHOULD BE INLET FLUSH WITH SURFACE

with wood in the long term. When the epoxy has cured, fillet the edges all round, to provide a finished look and to seal the vulnerable plywood edge from moisture.

Rudder Skegs. Rudder skegs are important in fast hulls to prevent blade flutter in the rudder and to provide better control at higher speed. They also protect the rudder from damage. Rudder skegs can also be reinforced using the same methods and should be adequately strong to withstand collision and to prevent damage to the rudder. Large (2-inch or 3-inch radius) structural epoxy fillets placed at the joint where the skeg meets the hull can be especially valuable for underwater streamlining and reinforcing. Such fillets should be mixed using mostly silica for high strength.

Shaping

Whether you're building or rebuilding, it is important to spend the necessary time shaping the underwater part of rudders and center-boards to the best airfoil possible. The leading edge of the blade should be a close match to the trailing edge of the keel, or, if the rudder is not attached to the after part of the keel, it should be airfoil-shaped from front to trailing edge. Whenever possible, hardware should be installed almost flush with the surface so that it does not protrude unnecessarily. Ideally, no part of the blade should be dead flat; there should be a slight camber, tapering from the leading to the trailing edge. The trailing edge should be slightly rounded, however; even though a sharp edge might furnish slightly better streamlining, it will get damaged much more easily.

Small plastic flaps attached to the trailing edge of the deadwood of the keel provide a flexible streamlining to the joint between keel and rudder, and are often helpful in preventing stalling or disturbance of the waterflow, especially in light airs. But you must take care not to provide an area where marine growth can flourish without your awareness. Any such flaps should be quite accessible for inspection and cleaning when the hull is hauled.

Part III
Flotation

How Much Flotation Do You Need?

On a simple, unballasted wood boat, positive flotation can be taken for granted. Otherwise, it's safer to assume that your boat comes equipped with negative flotation, also known as "positive sink." This option can be triggered by an unanticipated collision with a log or rock, a swamping from a wave or a knockdown, or just an undetected leak in the bilge. Before investing in a liferaft, consider this: No boat has to sink. By adding positive flotation in the form of foam, airtight compartments, or inflatable airbags, it is possible to keep any craft afloat.

Many small production boats come with factory-installed flotation, but it can be retrofitted into older hulls, too, and for good reason. An unsinkable hull provides a massive safety margin for any sailor. It allows the crew to stay with the boat, and its gear and supplies, until help arrives or the hole is patched and pumped out. If there is enough freeboard, it may even be possible to sail to port.

The total amount of flotation required to support a boat at the design waterline is roughly equal to the volume of the hull below the waterline. If you could somehow fill a boat with foam to the waterline, it would continue to float no matter how many holes there were in the hull. But the foam would take up so much interior space as to make a small boat unusable. The problem, therefore, is to provide the needed amount of flotation and not interfere with the living space or operation of the boat.

An easy way to estimate a boat's overall flotation requirement is to divide the loaded displacement in pounds by 64, the weight of one cubic foot of sea water. (Use 62 ½ pounds per cubic foot if you sail only in fresh water.) For instance, a boat with 1000 pounds displacement needs 15.6 cubic feet of flotation to be supported at the design waterline. This represents 100 percent of a boat's flotation need. Less than this amount will suffice if you also figure the flotation contribution made by the materials in the hull, deck, and interior, by enclosed tanks, cargo, and anything else that will float. Reductions of 30 to 70 percent of maximum are possible. Yet it is difficult if not dangerous to try to calculate the minimum amount of flotation. Always compensate on the safe side, provide backup protection in case one line of defense fails, and whenever possible test your calculations to see if your flotation ideas actually work.

Arrange flotation symmetrically fore and aft, port and starboard, to keep the hull balanced in case it floods.

Flotation Strategies

Foam

Foam is available in large quantities from professionals who spray trailer interiors and other structures for insulation, or it may be purchased in small aerosol cans. A catalyzed mixture of foam, poured or squirted into compartments, lockers, and other spaces would seem to be an ideal solution at first glance. Certainly it works, especially in small, isolated, or unused areas, but consider the drawbacks.

Poured-in-place foam is expensive. For a 30-foot boat we once built, a contractor quoted $800 for 80 cubic feet, and the price was just the beginning of the bad news. The contractor couldn't guarantee that the foam would not eventually break down and absorb water, and he had little or no information on the fumes it gave off, though he did seem to think it had a formaldehyde base. He also said there was danger of heat buildup while foaming the larger areas and that someone should stand by with fire extinguishers, just in case! We did eventually experiment with filling some small spaces with foam from aerosol cans and, true to expectations, it was not the best solution. The space could have been put to better use for multipurpose watertight compartments, which would have provided not only flotation but storage space, a valuable asset on small boats.

A good formulation of closed-cell foam blocks is another possibility, but valuable stowage space is being needlessly consumed.

There are other alternatives, however. For instance, flotation does not have to exist only in large, fixed chunks. Why not contain 50,000 ping-pong balls in a compartment or perhaps a fine mesh net? The ping-pong balls could be removed at any time for inspection, would never absorb water, and would conform to any shape!

Aside from ping-pong balls, there are non-absorbent, light-

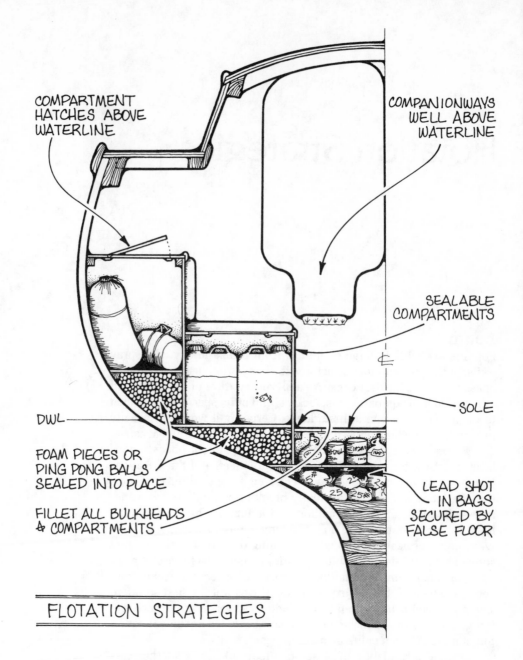

COMPARTMENT
HATCHES ABOVE
WATERLINE

COMPANIONWAYS
WELL ABOVE
WATERLINE

SEALABLE
COMPARTMENTS

SOLE

DWL

FOAM PIECES OR
PING PONG BALLS
SEALED INTO PLACE

FILLET ALL BULKHEADS
& COMPARTMENTS

LEAD SHOT
IN BAGS
SECURED BY
FALSE FLOOR

FLOTATION STRATEGIES

weight, and much less expensive materials available. Foam packing
"peanuts," so light they're hard to weigh, can be dumped into any
compartment and contained with a lid, door, or mesh net. They can
also be packed in plastic garbage bags and stuffed into odd corners.
A shop vacuum can be used to draw the air out of the bag; it will
also quickly empty a compartment of peanuts for cleaning or
inspection.

Foam peanuts provide a little less flotation than solid foam because of the space between the pieces, but a well-packed compartment will still add lots of buoyancy. There are dozens of different kinds, and you can experiment by squeezing, freezing, soaking them in salt water, and so on, to determine which work best. Best of all, packing material is cheap—and sometimes available almost for the asking from shipping departments. It does take time for the peanuts to settle and it may be necessary to keep adding more to top off a compartment, but the smaller sizes eventually pack quite tightly.

Compartments

If you wish to provide flotation and extra hull strength as well, you can divide the interior into a number of separate compartments, each with its own pumping system so you can deal with a leak or hole in one area while the rest of the boat stays dry. If it works as planned,

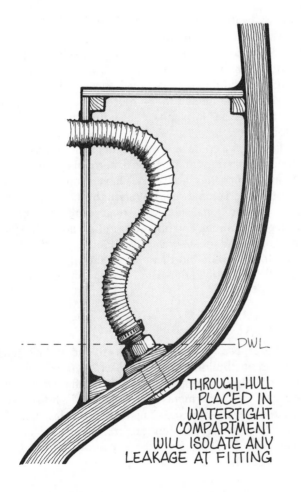

DWL

THROUGH-HULL
PLACED IN
WATERTIGHT
COMPARTMENT
WILL ISOLATE ANY
LEAKAGE AT FITTING

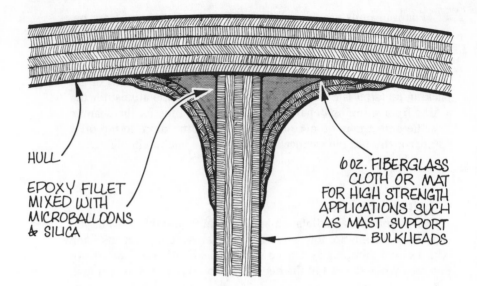

HULL

EPOXY FILLET
MIXED WITH
MICROBALLOONS
& SILICA

6 OZ. FIBERGLASS
CLOTH OR MAT
FOR HIGH STRENGTH
APPLICATIONS SUCH
AS MAST SUPPORT
BULKHEADS

compartmentalization allows time to think and gather your wits—time to deal efficiently with the problem.

A degree of compartmentalization can be achieved just by keeping the hatch cutouts in bulkheads as far above the design waterline as is practical. Dividing the bilge area into a series of watertight plywood compartments filleted to the hull will not only contain leaks and make them easier to combat, but will also serve as additional hull reinforcement.

Submarine-type doors and watertight crash bulkheads are a fine way to divide a boat into compartments, particularly in the vulnerable forepeak area. More than a few craft have limped into port with a flooded but sealed compartment. Watertight bulkheads are difficult to achieve in traditional plank-on-frame construction, but cold-molded, steel, aluminum, and fiberglass hulls readily lend themselves to this treatment. Adequate watertight doors are difficult and time-consuming to construct, but there are beautiful aluminum ones for large boats that fit into wood, glass, or metal bulkheads.

Sealed Tanks

Sealed multipurpose wood/epoxy tanks are one of the serendipitous refinements in boatbuilding during the last 20 years. Sheathed inside and out with 6-ounce fiberglass cloth and reinforced with epoxy fillets, these tanks can be permanently attached to the hull or be modular and easily removed. Compared to metal or fiberglass tanks, they are lightweight, long lasting, and don't suffer from rot or electrolysis. Best of all, they can be custom built for any application with common woodworking tools. Nearly every hull can benefit from some type of

Beckson screw-in deck plate. This transparent model allows visual inspection of locker contents—very handy for checking the presence of water in flotation or watertight compartments.

sealed tank, from underthwart or bow and stern tanks on a tiny pram to large-capacity sealed tanks on larger boats. Detailed building instructions will be found in Part V.

Sealed tanks are ideal for small boats because of their versatility. They can be filled with water, used until empty, and then sealed as flotation space. Sealed tanks can also hold gear and stores, providing dry storage and flotation at the same time they stiffen the hull.

With forethought, it is possible to incorporate these flotation chambers into underbunk areas, settee bottoms, and cabinetry where they will be virtually unnoticed. We struggled for years to design a watertight, easily removable, and easy-to-build hatch cover that would allow us access to our sealed compartments. Then we discovered the screw-in and pry-out deck plates made by Beckson Marine. These lightweight, round plates are easily installed with mounting screws or bolts and use an O-ring gasket and silicone sealant to make them truly watertight. We prefer the screw-in type, but the pry-outs probably work just as well and are available in slightly larger sizes. They can be removed and replaced in seconds. They are inexpensive, and can be placed on the top or the sides of compartments for access as needed. The deck plates with clear centers are ideal for dry storage lockers or for water tanks where the contents are fre-

Beckson screw-in deck plate, in black non-skid version, is good for sole, cockpit, or deck installations.

quently inspected. The covers should also be attached to a lanyard of some type, or to the chains available from Beckson.

Movable Ballast

If some ballast can be quickly and easily removed in an emergency, flotational requirements can be drastically reduced and the remaining flotation will support the hull higher in the water. Removable ballast could also help get you off if you're grounded (by loading a portion of ballast into a dinghy, then reloading after the keel comes free), can be used as trim to counteract excessive heel on one tack (useful for long passages in the trades), can compensate for uneven loading, or can be left ashore when cruising overloaded.

Boats that have large ballast casting, either bolted on the outside of the hull or sealed inside a glass hull, can use only limited amounts of removable ballast, if any. The idea works best on boats that have less than the maximum amount of ballast or don't have a fixed casting.

Movable ballast must be arranged in weights small enough to handle easily in a moving boat. Fifty-pound pigs, even with handles cast into them, are hard to maneuver in a pitching hull. They could also do a lot of damage if they got loose in rough weather. Ballast must be well secured when in place but capable of quick removal.

It's possible to bolt lead pigs in series to the deadwood—and this is a very secure method when properly done—but removing such ballast is tedious and usually requires the use of a ratcheting wrench.

One of the best choices for ballast is lead shot in 25- to 30-pound bags. The bags will conform to any odd nook and cranny, settling into places where a pickle jar wouldn't fit, and since a number of bags nestle together—they are surprising small—you can even protect vulnerable areas of the hull. The light weight of the bags allows them to be hoisted easily. For extra clean installations, the shot can be sealed in plastic bags, then plopped into canvas, burlap, or tarp bags and tied with a strong cord, leaving a hank of bagtop for a grip. Plastic bleach jugs filled with lead shot might also work, but because of their shape, they are difficult to fasten adequately in place.

Lead doesn't rust like boiler punchings and doesn't stain the bilge or wind up in a glob of oxidation. It is cheaper in shot form than as bars, ingots, or straps. You can scrounge wheel weights from service stations and tire shops and swap them to a metals dealer for lead shot, or if you have a band saw with an old blade, you can clamp lead wheel weights in a pair of Vise-Grips and cut them into marble-sized chunks yourself.

But make no mistake: although these bags stow well and seem to cling to the corners, they must be well contained in compartments and lockers with secure covers. They may cause less damage than a 50-pound bar careening around in the interior, but they would still be destructive if they got loose in very rough weather, just when you least need another problem.

For odd-shaped areas in the bilge where removable ballast might work, consider making lead shot plugs, which can be glued up with epoxy to any shape. This gives you a solid, custom-shaped piece of ballast without the need for melting lead or foundry services.

Airbags

Theoretically, you could achieve considerable flotation by stuffing your Avon inflatable into the cabin and pulling the inflation cord. While we're not really suggesting this seriously, it does open up an interesting avenue of possibility. Airbags could be an ideal approach to flotation since they are available "on demand" when the need for flotation arises and take up minimal cabin space when not in use. Low-lying airbags can provide the volume necessary to reduce the amount of water entering the boat. When the inside level reached the outside level, the leak would be much reduced or even stopped after a fashion. As with airbags for cars, however, this is no place for Rube Goldberg prototypes; simplicity and reliability are paramount.

Picture sausages of multi-celled raft material, or something similar, deflated and rolled into a tube and secured with Velcro straps alongside the sheer clamp, behind settees, and against the bulkheads.

They should be as low in the hull as possible—placed below the waterline if possible. CO_2 canisters could be used for inflation, but be sure to have spare foot pumps or hand pumps as a backup. When inflated, the airbags would be secured with trampoline netting or grommets and line, which would be rigged before inflation. Such a system would need regular inspection, and drills should be conducted—especially in the dead of night, when such devices might be most needed.

Backup Systems
The best way to develop confidence in your positive flotation is to rely on more than one type of flotation, to have as many backups and contingency plans as possible.

First, make everything aboard watertight. Start with major bulkheads and work down to smaller lockers and crannies. For instance, consider enclosing your through-hull fittings in sealed compartments extending well above the waterline. That way, if they spring a leak, they'll only fill their own compartment to the waterline. Become proficient in crafting strong epoxy fillets. They are the singlemost useful device when preparing a boat for built-in flotation.

Portable Pump Boards

Manually operated diaphragm pumps can move a lot of water, but they have to be fastened to something solid in order to provide the leverage to crank them efficiently. Sole- or bulkhead-mounted pumps work well, but what if you need a pump somewhere else in the boat, right away? What if you want to use the pump to wash the deck, or evacuate water from your tanks? Once you can move a pump around, many other uses will reveal themselves.

This "Guzzler" water pump and handle requires solid attachment to a pumpboard.

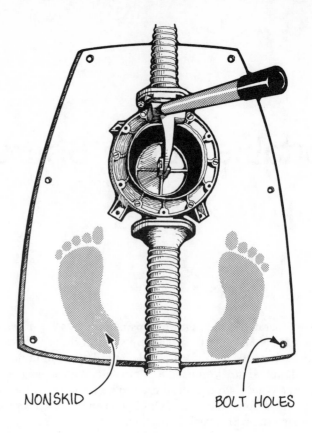

NONSKID   BOLT HOLES

A portable pump board gives you a surface on which to stand or kneel to hold the pump steady while you work the levers. The board can also be clamped or bolted to a bulkhead or sole if standing isn't possible.

The size of the board will vary according to the pumping force needed and where it's stowed. We usually make our boards from scraps of marine or hardwood plywood in various thicknesses from $\frac{3}{8}$ inch and up and trim their shape to fit where we wish to pump.

The boards will last a long time if you take the trouble to seal them with three coats of epoxy, paying particular attention to the edge grain. To keep the board from slipping around when you are pumping hard on a wet, slick surface, you can apply areas of non-skid on both bottom and top. Washed sand sprinkled into wet paint or epoxy is our favorite method, but it is too abrasive for use on gelcoat or a finely finished surface. A non-skid paint may be better in such places.

After you make the board, attach the pump and a length of hose on the intake and exhaust of the pump. Make sure you have adequate lengths of hose to reach out a port, into a self-draining cockpit or up through a deck hatch. For storage, you can drill a number of holes in the board and hang it on a hook in the forepeak or lay it on edge in the bilge. A patch or two of Velcro fastening will keep the handle in its place on the pump board, ready to use.

Part IV
Portlights, Hatches, and Lockers

Portlights

Portlights are a boater's window on the world. Tastefully designed and properly installed, they can complement a boat's personality, lower a visual profile, and even provide a look of forward movement. Below decks, portlights can add a feeling of spaciousness to sometimes cramped quarters, ventilating and lighting otherwise uninviting corners. A claustrophobic bunk can become, with the addition of an opening port, an enjoyable sanctuary with fresh air and a view.

Ports may be fitted anywhere—on cabin sides or tops, on decks, in the hull topsides, or even below the waterline for underwater sightseeing or picking a place to drop anchor. Whether you prefer the low, streamlined look of long, narrow ports or the traditional appeal of round or oval brass-framed ports, the challenge comes in choosing the appropriate style and sizes and placing the ports in an aesthetically pleasing manner.

Bronze, aluminum, and plastic ports of various shapes and sizes are readily available from suppliers. While bronze ports may look traditionally nautical, plastic ports have great advantages for small boats because they are lightweight and do not corrode or tarnish. They are also less expensive and available in a variety of styles and shapes, including both smoked and clear acrylics. They make ideal replacement ports in older boats and come complete with installation instructions. Beckson Marine (Box 3336, Bridgeport, CT 06605) supplies perhaps the most complete line of ports and accessories for small boats. It is also a fairly simple operation to make your own ports.

As a rule of thumb, smaller ports are usually safer on any boat exposed to occasional weather, and they don't compromise structural strength like large openings or slab-sided windows.

Safest of all—though they provide no ventilation—are sealed

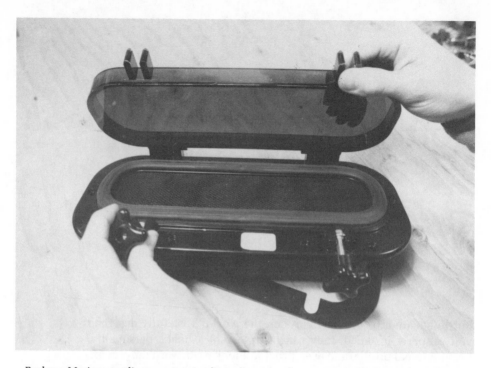

Beckson Marine supplies an extensive line of ports and accessories. The portlight shown here has a hinged cover with a removable mosquito net insert. Its smoked black finish offers privacy as well as a clean, modern look.

ports, or deadlights; they are also usually easier to install and stronger. Since they can never be accidentally left open, they can be installed in cabintops and on deck, but care must be taken to make them strong enough to withstand the occasional swat of a dropped winch handle or the load of foot traffic. They should also be made to fit flush, or at least equipped with a rounded edge or a bevel to prevent stubbed toes and snared lines.

Offshore boats should be equipped with hardwood braces for ports. Such braces can be temporary and fitted into place only when bad weather is expected, or they can be carefully fitted and finished and left in place. Large or suspect ports should have plywood storm shutters to fit them, and you should rig some method of attachment—screws, bolts, or lanyards—for each shutter.

Positioning the Ports

Locating a series of ports along a cabin side requires careful planning. The ports can follow the deck line, the cabintop, or any aesthetic combination of the boat's lines, as long as they look right. We experiment with positioning by using cardboard cutouts held temporarily in place with double-faced tape, and sometimes a long straight-

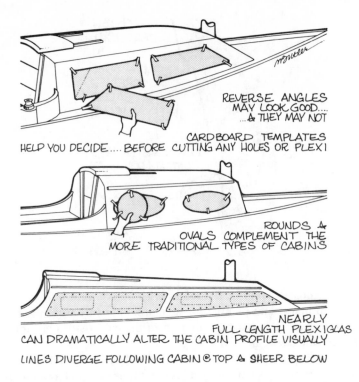

REVERSE ANGLES
MAY LOOK GOOD....
...& THEY MAY NOT

CARDBOARD TEMPLATES
HELP YOU DECIDE.... BEFORE CUTTING ANY HOLES OR PLEXI

ROUNDS &
OVALS COMPLEMENT THE
MORE TRADITIONAL TYPES OF CABINS

NEARLY
FULL LENGTH PLEXIGLAS
CAN DRAMATICALLY ALTER THE CABIN PROFILE VISUALLY

LINES DIVERGE FOLLOWING CABIN @ TOP & SHEER BELOW

edge or batten to maintain a fair line with the hull and cabin. Very small changes in position can make a lot of difference, so exercise care before cutting any holes. Be sure to look at the patterns from various angles. What may look good from aft or abeam will look skewed and sloppy from another view. In these cases, you must strike a compromise, or decide which angle of vision you wish to favor. Remember, most people will see the boat from abeam and from an elevated position.

It is also possible that there will be a conflict between the desired exterior look and your lighting or structural requirements below. For instance, openings are often needed in specific areas such as above the galley sink, over the chart table, or perhaps between cabintop beams and knees, but a series of little ports, asymmetrically installed, tends to give a cluttered look to the exterior. We have found that a single long piece of gray or smoked acrylic used to cover a number of openings in the cabin sides is often the answer. The appearance from outside the boat is of one long, narrow port; inside the boat, conveniently spaced openings provide light without compromising the structural integrity of the cabin sides.

Installing Ports

Ready-made opening ports are easy to install. Once you determine the size, shape, and location, all that's necessary is to cut the hole,

FLUSH
DEADLIGHT
IN
CABIN SIDE
SCREWED
& SEALED
WITH SILICONE

BLACK FASTENINGS
OFTEN LOOK BEST

PLEXIGLAS

CABIN
SIDES

seal the exposed wood or fiberglass with epoxy, and bolt or screw the port in place with plenty of fresh caulk to ensure watertightness. Be sure to leave a substantial margin of the cabin sides around the perimeter for fastening and strength.

Flush-fitting ports are a bit more work, but they provide a clean, finished look to decks or cabin sides. You'll need to cut a rabbet into the surface the same depth as the port. An alternate method, if the port is the same thickness as the deck or cabin side, is a backing plate or perimeter ring, epoxy glued for support. The backing plate or perimeter ring must be stout enough to support the port adequately under all conditions.

If you are concerned that your present ports are too big, making them smaller is entirely reasonable. In wood cabin sides, sealing off large holes is usually just a matter of carefully fitting quality plywood into the hole left by the removed port, then cutting a smaller hole in the plywood. The plywood should be inlet flush (see illustration). A strong backing block or cleat of some type may also be necessary to hold everything securely in place. After the hole is sealed, the new, smaller port is installed as a new construction.

TO DECREASE SIZE OF OPENING FOR A PORT

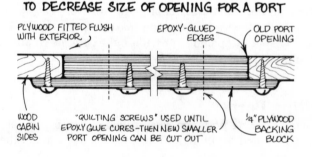

PLYWOOD FITTED FLUSH WITH EXTERIOR

EPOXY-GLUED EDGES

OLD PORT OPENING

WOOD CABIN SIDES

"QUILTING SCREWS" USED UNTIL EPOXY GLUE CURES—THEN NEW SMALLER PORT OPENING CAN BE CUT OUT

¼" PLYWOOD BACKING BLOCK

Fiberglass hulls usually require glassing over the hole left by the removed port. This requires building up a secure backing for the new laminate being applied over the hole. Again, plywood is an excellent material for backing and strengthening. Thinner laminations of plywood or wood veneer may be needed to conform to a rounded hull or cabin shape. If additional strength is needed, it may be necessary to attach a sawn or laminated rib or beam across the hole, either on the interior or possibly the exterior (see Part 2, under Exterior Beams).

Making Your Own Ports

For those who wish to design and build their own ports, acrylics such as Plexiglas and Lexan are ideal because they can be readily shaped using common woodworking tools. The careful application of heat from a portable propane torch will remove saw blade and router marks and replace a clear polished look to cut edges. *Caution*: *Keep the flame away from other parts of the port or it will distort vision through the port.*

Plexiglas is slightly flexible, especially in ⅛-inch thickness, but it stiffens with thickness and even a ¼-inch-thick port is quite stiff. For ports up to six inches across, ⅛-inch thickness is usually sufficient; larger ports (up to 18 inches across) will require ³⁄₁₆- or ¼-inch Plexiglas. In thicknesses of more than ¼-inch, Plexiglas gets very strong and heavy, and will work well for larger sized ports, greater than 18 inches across. We use ⁵⁄₁₆-inch and even ⅜-inch Plexiglas for these larger sizes, as well as for ports placed in vulnerable areas. Plexiglas sells for about $5 per square foot in ¼-inch thickness. Price increases with thickness.

The main drawback to Plexiglas is that it scratches rather easily, particularly with frequent handling. Fortunately, there are various polishes which may help cover the scratches. We have successfully used automotive wax (after a thorough washing) to cover small scratches, and others have had success with various brands of toothpaste. Beckson markets a two-part cleaner and polisher for plastic ports.

Lexan is similar to Plexiglas but is stronger and does not scratch nearly as easily. It sells for about double the cost of Plexiglas, about $9 to $10 per square foot for ¼-inch thickness. We follow the same thickness guidelines as for Plexiglas. Both acrylics are available clear or smoked. Smoked plastic looks much better from outside and also provides a degree of privacy below decks in daytime. When privacy is very important, such as over the head compartment, Plexiglas and Lexan may be sanded to a translucent finish using a belt or orbital sander and 150-grit sandpaper.

Shatterproof automotive safety glass is another option. A ¼-inch-thick piece sells for about $7 per square foot. Glass has superior hardness and scratch resistance and could be an ideal material for home-

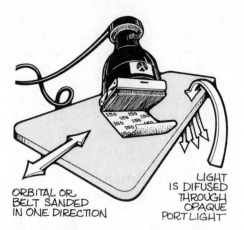

ORBITAL OR
BELT SANDED
IN ONE DIRECTION

LIGHT
IS DIFUSED
THROUGH
OPAQUE
PORTLIGHT

built ports and windows, except that shaping, cutting, and drilling usually require the services of a professional glass shop. Sandblasting is required for a translucent finish since the glass is too hard to sand (smoked safety glass is available). Safety glass has other drawbacks as well. The rubber channel molding used to mount safety glass is not usually supportive or positive enough for use on boats exposed to rough water (rubber channel requires supportive braces on the backside should it fail), and the fastening holes drilled near the edge can easily exert enough force to break the glass.

With any of these materials, use particular care with drilling and tightening fastenings near the edges. Roundhead screws or bolts are the best methods of attachment because they exert a steady, flat force on the surface. The wedge shape of a flathead wood screw exerts sideways pressure that will break out corners if overtightened. For areas where more force is needed, a washer will help spread the strain

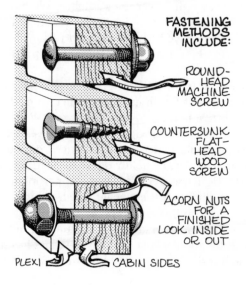

FASTENING
METHODS
INCLUDE:

ROUND-
HEAD
MACHINE
SCREW

COUNTERSUNK
FLAT-
HEAD
WOOD
SCREW

ACORN NUTS
FOR A
FINISHED
LOOK INSIDE
OR OUT

PLEXI   CABIN SIDES

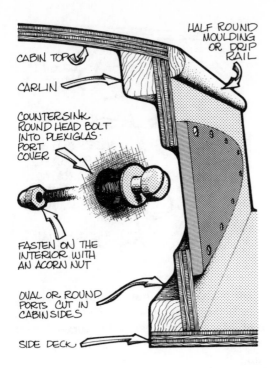

CABIN TOP

CARLIN

COUNTERSINK
ROUND HEAD BOLT
INTO PLEXIGLAS
PORT
COVER

HALF ROUND
MOULDING
OR DRIP
RAIL

FASTEN ON THE
INTERIOR WITH
AN ACORN NUT

OVAL OR ROUND
PORTS CUT IN
CABIN SIDES

SIDE DECK

of fastening. Holes drilled for fastenings should be slightly oversize and sealed with caulking. Silicone is an excellent sealant and bedding for ports, regardless of size or type. Apply a substantial bead around the perimeter of the port to ensure a complete and uniform seal. (If you are installing acrylic portlights, you can watch the sealant fill the seam as the fastenings are tightened.) Though the fastenings may tighten easily, take care not to force all sealant out of the joint. Portlight materials shrink and swell with changes in temperature, and if the caulking or sealant is too thin it breaks instead of stretching.

Excess sealant can be trimmed once it cures slightly. You can also form a small fillet in fresh silicone with your finger (wear a rubber glove) or with a round-ended wood tongue depressor. Work fast because silicone cures quickly and will only stay pliable enough to form a fillet for a few minutes. Don't pester silicone after it starts to harden. Leave it alone and come back later with a sharp knife or razor to trim the excess.

Sliding and Hinged Ports

Sliding ports are not completely watertight and are probably an unwise choice for craft that will ever have to venture into rough water. In sheltered waters, however, they can work well on small boats if properly designed and installed. They are adjustable for ventilation, take up no extra room when open or closed, and are easily built once

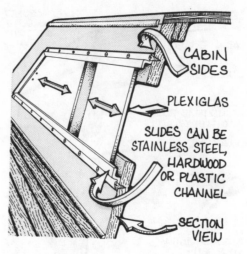

CABIN SIDES

PLEXIGLAS

SLIDES CAN BE STAINLESS STEEL, HARDWOOD OR PLASTIC CHANNEL

SECTION VIEW

the materials are on hand. Sliding windows sometimes consist of three or more sections of glass or acrylic, but most are just two panes with a 3-inch or 4-inch overlap across the center. The panes should be longer than they are tall in order to slide properly, without jamming or sticking.

The slides or track for sliding windows are available in stainless steel, aluminum, and plastic, or you can make them yourself out of epoxy-glued hardwood. Beckson sells double- and triple-channel tracks designed for the do-it-yourselfer. The best channels use a double groove to separate the panes of acrylic so they won't scratch as they slide past each other. Felt or gasket material placed between or inside the slides provides the necessary friction and sound deadening. For opening and closing sliders, you can mill a slight indentation for a finger grip using a table saw blade carefully set to half the thickness of the acrylic, or by simply attaching a teak strip to the acrylic with

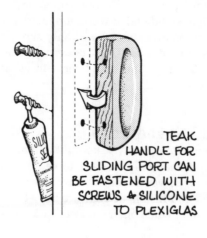

TEAK HANDLE FOR SLIDING PORT CAN BE FASTENED WITH SCREWS & SILICONE TO PLEXIGLAS

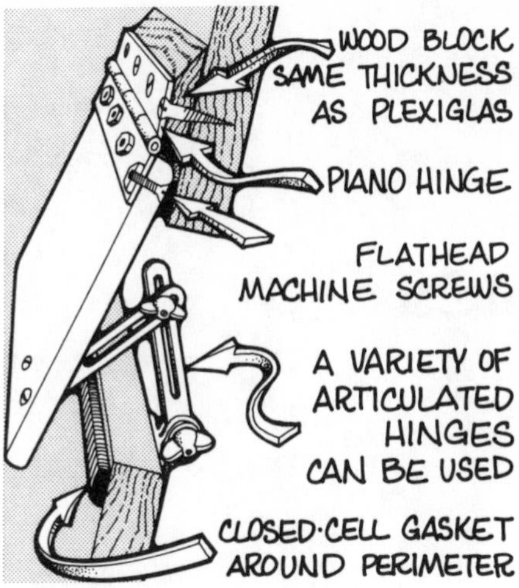

WOOD BLOCK
SAME THICKNESS
AS PLEXIGLAS

PIANO HINGE

FLATHEAD
MACHINE SCREWS

A VARIETY OF
ARTICULATED
HINGES
CAN BE USED

CLOSED-CELL GASKET
AROUND PERIMETER

screws from the outside. The windows can be held open or closed with shock cord or a more positive hook closure.

The shape of a sliding window is determined somewhat by what you can achieve with your perimeter moldings and sliders. A streamlined round or sloping angle looks best but may require tedious molding work. One alternative is to provide simple stops fore and aft and use track or plastic channel only on the top and bottom.

Hinged ports may not be the most nautical type of opening, but they can be made much tighter than a sliding port. Also, unlike the more traditional portlights, hinged ports can provide good ventilation during a rain, and since no moldings are required, they can be any shape or configuration without much extra work. Where structural strength is required, a piano hinge is the best method of attachment.

Hatches

Complete Hatch Units

Installing a hatch unit in a foredeck or cabintop where none has previously existed can have numerous benefits on a small boat. An extra hatch can provide improved ventilation, more light, and more convenient access to the inside and outside of the boat. It will make stowing and retrieving gear easier and provide an additional exit from the boat in case of an emergency.

A hatch unit consists of two main components: the hatchcover (including top and sides) and the coamings, the four pieces that form the framework for the hatch. It is possible to build a hatch by assembling the coamings, support cleats, sides, and cover right on the boat, but a better approach is to build and finish the complete unit before installing it. This method is much easier, and chances are you will end up with a much stronger and better-looking hatch. It is much simpler to keep the coamings perfectly square or do any fancy joining when building on a solid, flat workbench where you'll have the pieces and tools you'll need close at hand. Care in building yields a good fit, which along with proper sealing, gaskets, and a secure latch is an important factor in watertightness.

While teak is a traditional favorite of boatbuilders, hatchcovers do not necessarily have to be made of expensive hardwoods. Spruce and fir also make fine, lightweight, and inexpensive hatches. Although it looks quite untraditional, high-quality hardwood plywood also makes excellent coamings and hatchcover components when sealed with epoxy. In fact, plywood is the material of choice for the top, because once fitted it has the necessary stability to hold its shape for years. The boatowner who wants to spend more time sailing and less time maintaining his or her boat will glue and seal the wood with epoxy and paint over it. Protected in this fashion, the surface will last for years without maintenance of any kind—much longer than coamings and hatchtops finished bright.

Assembly

The first step in building your hatch is to plan where you intend to install it. If there are deck or cabintop beams, have the hatch lie between two beams if possible, using the beams as support and reinforcement. If you can't arrange to lay the hatch between two beams, then use at least one beam against the forward or after coaming to secure the hatch structure. With some small boats, you may need to cut through a beam to make the hatch opening large enough. This is usually no problem as long as the hatch coamings are well secured to the deck and to the remaining beam so they make up for the loss of beam strength.

On a glass deck, it is preferable to locate a hatch reasonably close to a structural bulkhead if possible: if not, the unit can be placed anywhere convenient. If the unit is properly built and installed, it will provide additional structural support for the deck.

A hatch used for stowage or as a passageway should be at least large enough to accommodate your shoulders with your arms at your sides, even if only on the diagonal. Hatches used exclusively for ventilation can be any size and placed in the most advantageous locations. The coamings should project at least an inch above the deck level—sometimes more depending on the size of the boat, the camber (curve) of the deck, and the location of the hatch. When planning a hatch, keep in mind that the hole cut in the deck or cabintop will need to be cut slightly larger than the actual desired opening size to allow for the coamings.

The wood pieces used for coamings must be straight, not warped or twisted. Quarter-sawn wood has superior long-term stability, as does high-quality plywood. Assemble the coamings using long sliding clamps, and keep a framing square handy to ensure that the coam-

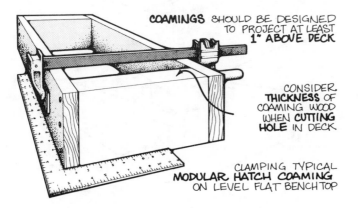

COAMINGS SHOULD BE DESIGNED TO PROJECT AT LEAST 1" ABOVE DECK

CONSIDER THICKNESS OF COAMING WOOD WHEN CUTTING HOLE IN DECK

CLAMPING TYPICAL MODULAR HATCH COAMING ON LEVEL FLAT BENCHTOP

ings don't rack (get out of square) as you fasten and glue. The best way to avoid building a racked coaming is to use simple butt joints and keep the coaming end cuts square and straight. But if, in spite of your best efforts, the coamings go out of square as you fasten them, put a long sliding clamp diagonally across the coaming, and use light clamping pressure to pull the coaming square while the glue dries. If the coaming is still slightly out of square after the glue has dried, all is not lost, but the remedy will have to await the installation stage. At that time, it may be possible to force the coaming into a perfectly square-cut hole in the deck using a few small wedges between the edge of the hole and the coaming. Cleats (small wood support members) or epoxy fillets will then hold the frame square and complete the installation.

There are various ways to join the coaming pieces or sides of the hatchtop together, including fancy dovetails, square half laps, miter joints, and simple butt joints. If you plan on finishing bright, seal the screw holes in the ends of the coamings with matching wood plugs. If you're painting, microballoon-thickened epoxy is actually best for sealing and will provide good protection to the fastenings.

Once the coaming unit is assembled—and provided it is square—you can lay out the hatchcover right on top of it. The amount of clearance between the coamings and sides of the cover is determined in part by the height of the coamings: more height requires more clearance to open and close without rubbing or sticking. Spacers of ⅟₁₆- inch or ⅛-inch-thick plastic laminate or wood veneer

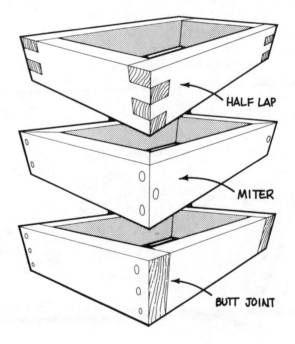

HALF LAP

MITER

BUTT JOINT

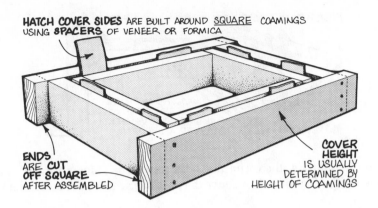

HATCH COVER SIDES ARE BUILT AROUND <u>SQUARE</u> COAMINGS USING **SPACERS** OF VENEER OR FORMICA

ENDS ARE **CUT OFF SQUARE** AFTER ASSEMBLED

COVER HEIGHT IS USUALLY DETERMINED BY HEIGHT OF COAMINGS

placed between the coaming and the side pieces when laying out the cover will ensure adequate clearance in most applications.

Build the side pieces of the hatchcover first; once they are assembled with proper clearance, attach the top. The top can be glued and screwed right onto the tops of the side pieces, or a small rabbet can be cut to fit the top flush (a rabbet will also seal the end grain if the top is plywood). A router with a carbide rabbet bit will quickly cut a perfect groove for the top. For hatchcovers 18 inches by 18 inches or smaller, ⅜-inch-thick plywood is sufficient. Wider hatchtops may need ⁷⁄₁₆-inch or even ½-inch-thick plywood. To determine the appropriate thickness, lay a piece across the frame and stand on it. If it doesn't flex too much, it will probably work just fine.

For see-through hatchtops, use an acrylic sheet at least ¼-inch thick—considerably thicker for larger boats and larger hatchcovers. Keep in mind the consequences if the hatchtop should break, and don't skimp on its thickness. Lexan is tougher than Plexiglas and probably a better choice for deck and cabintop hatchcovers that may get stepped on and have winch handles dropped on them. A liberal application of silicone sealant will waterproof the edges and provide a flexible gasket, providing the acrylic is not fastened too tightly.

The sides of the hatchcover will most likely have to be trimmed to the shape of the deck or cabintop after the coaming is installed. Transfer the camber of the deck or cabintop to the hatchcover sides

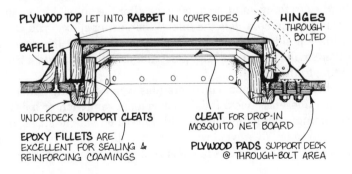

PLYWOOD TOP LET INTO **RABBET** IN COVER SIDES

HINGES THROUGH-BOLTED

BAFFLE

UNDERDECK **SUPPORT CLEATS**

EPOXY FILLETS ARE EXCELLENT FOR SEALING & REINFORCING COAMINGS

CLEAT FOR DROP-IN MOSQUITO NET BOARD

PLYWOOD PADS SUPPORT DECK @ THROUGH-BOLT AREA

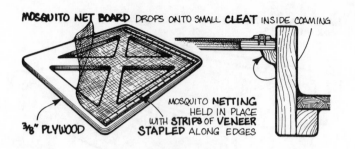

MOSQUITO NET BOARD DROPS ONTO SMALL CLEAT INSIDE COAMING

MOSQUITO NETTING HELD IN PLACE WITH STRIPS OF VENEER STAPLED ALONG EDGES

3/8" PLYWOOD

with a compass, then trim the sides to fit. The sides normally rest against the coamings just above the deck surface, not flat on the deck.

Installation

After all pieces are built, it's time for installation. Lay the assembled unit on the deck and cut the hole to match. If necessary, drill pilot holes up from the interior to show the location of beams. Allow about ⅛ inch all around for sealing the fiberglass laminate or wood grain of the deck or cabintop. Epoxy creates the best seal, but caulking also works well and may be applied under and over the tops of support cleats (see ahead).

When the hatch is clamped into its permanent location in the deck or cabintop, install the support cleats (shown in the illustration on page 107), or use epoxy fillets to hold the hatch structure in place. Epoxy fillets are easier and do a better job of both holding and sealing, but wood cleats also work well and look good, although they sometimes require considerable trimming and bending to fit the underside of the deck or cabintop.

Wood cleats usually are fastened to both the underside of the deck and the sides of the coamings with wood screws. Phillips head screws allow you to work more easily in cramped positions. Be sure to predrill with the proper sized bit to prevent splitting the wood. The ends of cleats can be butted, or you can fit a fancy miter joint if you wish.

When using epoxy fillets as structural supports, fill the space with thickened epoxy and form a pleasing fillet on the visible sides. If the coaming is clamped in place, apply a few small "tack" fillets to hold everything solid, then go back after the epoxy kicks, remove the clamps, and complete the fillet. When using epoxy, you can also seal the top side of the coamings, where they meet the deck, with another small fillet. It will seal the seam and also provide a finished molding to the joint.

There are additional considerations when installing hatch coamings in a fiberglass deck. If the deck is foam sandwich or balsa core, the coamings should be particularly well sealed or bedded, especially on the top edges, to prevent water from soaking into the foam or balsa. And for a single-layer glass hull it is vitally important to make a strong

Interior-mounted locking mechanisms, such as the one pictured here, allow you to adjust the pressure on the hatchcover by turning the bolt.

structural connection between the hatch coaming and the deck with screws, bolts, and beddings and/or epoxy.

After the coaming is in place, all that remains is to fit the hatchtop in place and attach the hinges. Hinging arrangements are diverse and include traditional hatch hinges, piano hinges, and special types that have removable pins, which allow a hatch to pivot from various sides for better ventilation. All these types are available from marine stores or mail order suppliers of marine hardware.

Some fine tuning always seems necessary for new hatches. A small rasp or even sandpaper on a block will remove small amounts of wood from any spots where the cover is rubbing against the coaming. Leave the hatch in place for a month or so to settle in; and then go back over it one more time to fine tune opening, closing, and locking.

Locking Mechanisms for Hatches

Most hatches have their locking mechanisms on the inside of the boat, except for the companionway hatch, which usually can be locked from either inside or outside.

Interior locking mechanisms are usually easy to install. A hook and eyelet is about the simplest possible arrangement, as long as it doesn't rattle or vibrate. Brass hooks look good and can be bent slightly with a pair of pliers to create a tight fit. The best system is usually to attach the eyelet to the hatch cover or the moving part of the structure and attach the hook to the coaming so it will lie quietly alongside the coaming when not in use.

Adjustable mechanisms for locking a hatch from the interior are also available and allow you to vary the pressure on the hatchcover by turning a bolt. If the coamings are of sufficient height and thickness to take the required fastenings, these types are very handy and can adjust the pressure to a gasket. They do, however, project into the hatch somewhat and restrict the size of the opening, so they might not be the best choice for small-sized openings.

Companionway Hatches

The companionway hatch on small decked boats is generally a two-part structure—a vertical opening through the cockpit bulkhead and a horizontal opening extending forward onto the deck or cabintop allowing a person to walk down the companionway steps and forward into the cabin with as little crouching and contortion as possible. Hatchboards and a sliding hatchcover make the unit watertight and lockable. The companionway is by far the biggest opening to the interior of a boat, and its design is especially important because of the number of factors that must be considered.

First and foremost is safety at sea. The companionway hatch should be as high above the waterline as is practical to prevent water from slopping aboard and downflooding the interior, and the bottom of the lowest hatchboard should be elevated at least a few inches above cockpit level (preferably a self-draining cockpit) to keep run-off and splash out of the cabin.

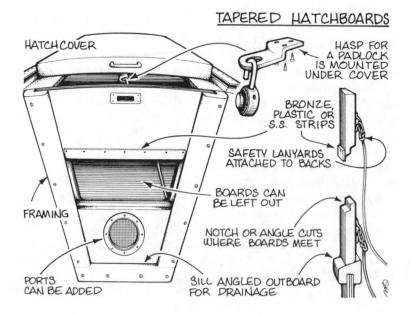

TAPERED HATCHBOARDS

HATCHCOVER

HASP FOR A PADLOCK IS MOUNTED UNDER COVER

BRONZE, PLASTIC OR S.S. STRIPS

SAFETY LANYARDS ATTACHED TO BACKS

BOARDS CAN BE LEFT OUT

FRAMING

NOTCH OR ANGLE CUTS WHERE BOARDS MEET

PORTS CAN BE ADDED

SILL ANGLED OUTBOARD FOR DRAINAGE

The companionway hatch is often a boat's primary ventilation, so it should also be designed for maximum comfort in hot weather. Sometimes the hatch has to provide ventilation and keep out bugs or rain at the same time. In order for the cabin to be usable while the hatchboards and cover are in place, there must be a means of allowing light to enter.

An additional concern of companionway hatch design is convenient access. Going below for an anchor stowed in the forepeak, for another quick look at the chart and tide tables before you enter a passage, or for a cup of hot tea to get you through the last of your watch, might mean that you enter and exit the hatch dozens of times in the course of a day. You'll use it in rough weather, wet weather, and dark of night, so you want to make the passageway the right size and, with its hatchboards and cover, as easily and quickly adjustable as possible.

The combination of all these competing concerns, plus the fact that space is almost always at a premium on small boats, often produces creative, multipurpose companionway hatches and hatchcovers. In short, how well a companionway hatch performs its functions—opening and closing, ventilating, lighting, providing a view from below, and keeping everything dry and secure—has much to do with the success and livability of the boat itself.

Companionway hatches traditionally are tapered openings. The tapered shape, plus gravity, will hold each hatchboard in its place. Besides, tapered hatchboards are one of the simplest ways to provide a positive closure and a degree of adjustability. They are inexpensive and easier to build than louvered or hinged doors, and they also provide a degree of durability and safety that other types of doors never achieve.

In the interest of safety, keep the hatch opening size as small as possible; even an 18-inch top opening is usable if you learn to turn slightly sideways as you enter and exit. The bottom of the tapered opening can be quite small, since your feet usually go through one at a time.

Hatchboards

Hatchboard thickness depends on the size of the boat and the dimensions of the opening. For heavier hulls, ¾-inch-thick hardwoods like teak, mahogany, or iroko may be appropriate for hatchboards, while smaller, lighter hulls can use smaller sizes. Quality hardwood plywood is much stronger than timber for the same weight and is less prone to splitting and warping. We use ¼-inch plywood only for the smallest openings; ⅜-inch to ½-inch plywood is considerably stiffer and safer. If you want to be completely sure, cut a sample board and check to be sure that it doesn't flex.

Plywood for hatchboards must be well sealed on the edges,

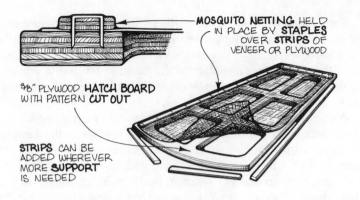

MOSQUITO NETTING HELD IN PLACE BY **STAPLES** OVER **STRIPS** OF VENEER OR PLYWOOD

⅜" PLYWOOD **HATCH BOARD** WITH PATTERN **CUT OUT**

STRIPS CAN BE ADDED WHEREVER MORE **SUPPORT** IS NEEDED

which means three coatings of epoxy, and paint or sunscreen protection over the epoxy. Thus treated, the boards almost never warp.

For spanning a hatch closure of approximately three feet or wider, timber strips screwed and glued to the front or back side of the plywood hatchboards will increase stiffness. Exterior strips should have their top edges tapered or shaped so they don't hold water from rain or spray and cause a possible pocket for rot. A small epoxy fillet on the topside will also solve the problem.

Hatchboards can be held in place on the cockpit bulkhead by a variety of methods, from fancy mitered teak moldings with matching plugs over the fastenings to simple stainless steel or aluminum channels bolted to the bulkhead. The moldings must be self-draining (with the bottoms left open or drain holes drilled) so water will not pool. If you fit a hardwood sill or step across the bottom of the cutout, it should be angled outboard—again, to provide drainage. For a snug fit, carefully cut the bottom hatchboard at the same angle as the sill.

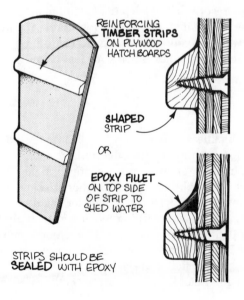

REINFORCING **TIMBER STRIPS** ON PLYWOOD HATCH BOARDS

SHAPED STRIP

OR

EPOXY FILLET ON TOP SIDE OF STRIP TO SHED WATER

STRIPS SHOULD BE **SEALED** WITH EPOXY

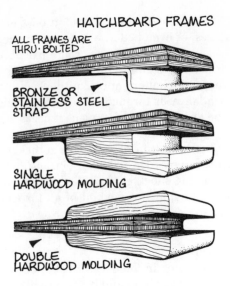

HATCHBOARD FRAMES

ALL FRAMES ARE
THRU·BOLTED

BRONZE OR
STAINLESS STEEL
STRAP

SINGLE
HARDWOOD MOLDING

DOUBLE
HARDWOOD MOLDING

Also cut the bottoms and tops of adjoining hatchboards at a slight angle to allow wind-driven spray, rain, and dew to drain outboard. A 30-degree outboard-sloping cut is sufficient. For additional protection and reinforcement, you can add a thin strip of bronze or brass to the seam between hatchboards, always attaching the strip to the bottom of the hatchboard. This looks good and will improve alignment on thin, wide hatchboards. Another approach, particularly appropriate for thinner hatchboards, is to make half laps, with the top lap (the one at the bottom of the upper board) to the outside, as in the illustration on page 110. The laps provide additional stiffness, lessening the chance of gaps forming between the boards, but they are much harder to cut properly.

The hatchboards should be cut slightly wider than the hatch and worked carefully into position, one at a time, from bottom to top, using a block plane. If you cut too much the boards will rattle, but they should not be so tight that they stick in place. If in the process of fitting you cut too much off the sides, causing the board to drop too far in the slot or become loose, remove a thin slice from the bottom and refit the sides. (That's why you should leave some extra wood at the top of the topmost hatchboard and make the final cut only after all the other boards are fitted in place.)

Installing one or more plastic-framed Beckson ports into the hatchboards has numerous advantages. Fitted with screens to keep bugs out, such ports provide ventilation, light, and a convenient view from the cabin. They are lightweight, very simple to install, and come in such a variety of sizes that even the smallest hatchboard usually has sufficient room to accommodate one.

Although correct shaping and gravity are normally sufficient to hold the hatchboards in place, additional safety is gained by tethering each board to the boat, as in the illustration on page 110. It's also wise to carry spares, or even better, a one-piece emergency replacement. You can easily make a one-piece spare hatchboard of quality plywood and stow it flat against a bulkhead, under a bunk or settee cushions, or even in the bottom of cockpit lockers. Attach a couple of strong tiedown lanyards through small holes in the spare hatchboard so it can be quickly secured in place if necessary. One-eighth-inch lace line works well and can be knotted on either side of the spare hatchboard to keep it in place. Leave sufficient length of line on each end to reach a cleat or tiedown point inside and outside the cabin. A loop of strong shock cord hooked inside and outside also works well and is the quickest method of all for attaching and releasing a hatchboard.

Sliding Hatchcovers

The companionway hatch in the deck or cabintop usually is closed by a sliding hatchcover on tracks and runners, which keeps the water out, and also provides the base for locking the entire hatch. When the hatchcover is closed, a simple brass or stainless steel tab projects through a slot cut in the top hatchboard to attach a padlock. There are other ways to lock a companionway hatch, but none is simpler to build, stronger, or much more effective. If you wish to dress up the locking system a bit, you can also fit a small square plate of matching metal flush around the slot in the hatchboard, giving it a traditional touch and protecting the wood from the lock.

A sliding hatchcover that jams will drive you crazy, so it's best to build it right the first time around. If possible, make the runners (which support the tracks) out of epoxy-glued laminated wood sections; these are always more stable than a large single piece of timber. Be sure the tracks and runners are parallel to each other, that they provide enough clearance to slide smoothly in all weather, and that

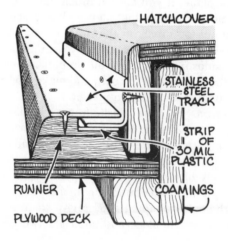

1" x 1½" HIGH - GLUED &
SCREWED TO DECK

IF NEEDED,
A WOOD BAFFLE
FORWARD OF SLIDING HATCH
WILL PREVENT EXCESSIVE AMOUNTS
OF WATER ENTERING DUE TO WIND OR WAVES...... .

they are snug enough not to rattle. One secret for a smooth-working hatch is a strip of thick plastic (30-mil, or ⅛-inch thick) on the bearing surface for the hatch slides. Such plastic is tough, longlasting, not affected by salt water, and works equally well in tropical sun or when frozen solid. The strip may be predrilled and fastened with bronze ring nails or with flathead screws countersunk flush or just slightly below the surface.

Sometimes on small boats, wind will drive spray and wavetops over the deck and force water under the hatchcover, over the coamings, and into the cabin. Baffles around the hatch will prevent this from happening. If such baffles are used, provide drain holes in the corners or leave the corners open so water will not pool. Finally, to negate the danger of a hatch suddenly sliding closed as it might if the boat pounds or lurches, the sliding hatch should also be provided with some type of positive stop to hold it open. A simple hook and eyelet will work well.

Self-draining Lockers and Compartments

Compartments regularly exposed to rain and spray can be made self-draining so that water does not accumulate inside. Cockpit lockers, deck boxes, anchor lockers, and other places aboard a small boat are ideal candidates for such self-draining compartments. We kept a small Honda generator, an outboard motor, and its fuel tank in a draining cockpit locker for years and were convinced that it was the best possible location for these items on a small boat. The cockpit was often wet from spray and rain, but the locker dried without attention and was easy to keep clean.

To ensure that water doesn't pool in the compartment, drain holes should be located at each corner so the space will drain completely regardless of the attitude or loading of the boat. Be sure that the bottom of the compartment slopes toward the holes. Drain holes don't have to be as large as cockpit scuppers, which must empty in a hurry, but they should be flush with the sole of the compartment,

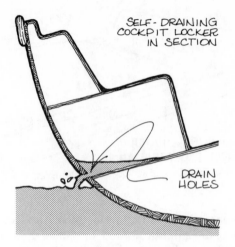

SELF-DRAINING
COCKPIT LOCKER
IN SECTION

DRAIN
HOLES

or half-moon shaped, and their edges should be well sealed with epoxy.

Cockpit lockers usually drain inboard onto the cockpit sole, which delivers the water to the cockpit scuppers and overboard. They can also drain outboard, through the hull or the transom, as long as the drain holes can be located far enough above the waterline, so the locker can't fill from outside during routine sailing. Divide these cockpit lockers from the rest of the boat with watertight bulkheads.

Plank-on-frame hulls should have all such compartments and drain holes well sealed, and resealed on a regular basis, to prevent rot. Cold-molded and fiberglass hulls can easily avoid this problem with a liberal application of epoxy seal to all surfaces. Fiberglass cloth sheathing on the bottoms of compartments improves abrasion resistance, strength, and durability—a well-sealed compartment with sheathing and epoxy fillets in the corners will last for years without any maintenance. Compartments that are normally closed will shield the epoxy from ultraviolet degradation, but painted locker interiors look good, are easier to keep clean, and protect the epoxy better.

Anchor Lockers

A self-draining locker in the forepeak greatly simplifies the otherwise clumsy but essential task of stowing the anchor and its chain. The locker can also hold items like fenders and line that might be useful in a hurry. Such forepeak lockers can be built with epoxy-sealed plywood and covered with flush-fitting hatchtops to keep the deck smooth. If the sides of the anchor locker extend right out to the hull sides, the locker requires only a bottom, back, and front. A drainage hole on each side of the hull will do the job if the locker bottom is sloped slightly toward them. Lightweight plastic through-hull fittings

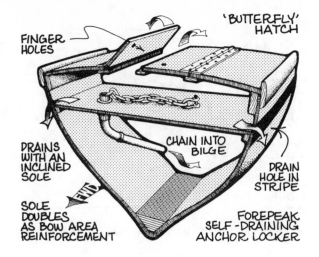

FINGER HOLES

'BUTTERFLY' HATCH

DRAINS WITH AN INCLINED SOLE

CHAIN INTO BILGE

FWD

DRAIN HOLE IN STRIPE

SOLE DOUBLES AS BOW AREA REINFORCEMENT

FOREPEAK SELF-DRAINING ANCHOR LOCKER

work well for these installations because they are inexpensive and easy to shape and install. They can also be made less noticeable if placed in a sheer stripe or under a trailboard.

Plastic or PVC pipe can be used as a hawsepipe to lead the anchor chain down into the bilge, where it contributes helpful additional ballast. The diameter of the pipe should be large enough to enable the chain links to turn in any direction without kinking as they slip through.

Bronze or stainless steel piano hinges are ideal for two-piece "butterfly" hatchcovers in the forepeak deck. Since the area is often wet from spray, the fastening screws should be dipped in a drop of epoxy before final insertion. Stainless steel self-tapping screws are good fasteners for glass decks and may also be inserted into wood cleats below the deck.

For smaller-sized hatches and one-piece hatchtops, the usual underdeck cleats on the perimeter usually provide the necessary support. (Epoxy-glued plywood is best for these underdeck supports because it can be cut to any shape without regard for grain orientation and will not split as easily as timber cleats.) Larger hatches may need a centerline support to reinforce each half cover. If this breaks up the opening too much (defeating the purpose of a large hatch), you can solve the problem by attaching the support to one of the half covers rather than to the coaming, as in the accompanying illustration. Drill finger holes to provide a means of lifting the top, or install one of the various types of flush-fitting hardware with a lifting ring or handle, readily available from marine hardware suppliers. Remember, these hatches also have to be secured against coming open. Various types of closure hardware are available, or you can make underdeck toggles that can be manipulated through finger holes (see page 132). If you use this system, you should also secure it with a safety line.

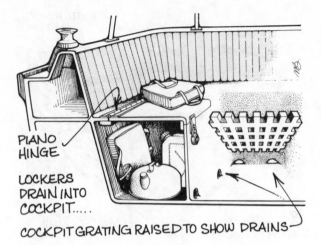

PIANO HINGE

LOCKERS DRAIN INTO COCKPIT.....

COCKPIT GRATING RAISED TO SHOW DRAINS

Securing Lockers and Compartments

Cockpit lockers, lazarettes, on-deck gear boxes, and foredeck anchor lockers all need a means by which their covers can be held securely in place. This should be an important design consideration in all new construction, but sometimes it is a necessary retrofit as well. For example, in many of today's production minicruisers, cockpit lockers with flush-fitting covers open directly onto quarter berths below. If a following sea should break in the cockpit, or a knockdown should occur, dislodging the covers, serious downflooding of the cabin could occur. Back at the mooring, a sturdy lock is also a sensible precaution against break-ins.

The above illustration shows a typical latching system for a cockpit locker, using a piano hinge and a padlock. When installing locking mechanisms in the cockpit, try to move it to the edges or sides of the locker, leaving the top clear for sitting.

Serious locking mechanisms are commonly backed up with plywood backing blocks and fastened with machine screws and nuts or even heavy-duty bolts. Antivibration nuts, such as Nylok, can be used to advantage if they are available, or a dab of silicone seal can be applied to the nut end of a bolt to keep it from vibrating off. Screws are rarely used to attach locking hardware, although the excellent square-drive Robertson head screws can usually be considered secure because so few people have square-head drivers to remove them.

Part V
Interior Stowage and Creature Comforts

Ceilings, Hull Liners, and Insulation

A bare, single-skin fiberglass or metal boat is like a house without insulation. In cold weather, warmth lasts only until the heater is turned off and condensation hangs in drops overhead and trickles down the hull sides. In hot weather, the hull becomes a sauna as soon as the sun hits it. The acoustics are only slightly better than living in a 50-gallon steel drum, and the interior always seems to smell like resin, rust or mildew.

Thin wood hulls also benefit from an insulating and sound-absorbing ceiling or hull liner. And such liners can add to the structural strength, attractiveness, safety, and comfort of many small boats, regardless of material.

Traditional Ceilings

A typical ceiling treatment for wood boats uses 3-inch wide strips, usually spruce, pine, or fir (and occasionally hardwoods like mahogany or teak), screwed to the ribs with a $\frac{1}{4}$-inch to 1-inch space between the edges for circulation. To make ceiling strips, we usually rip $\frac{3}{4}$-inch thick planks into 3-inch widths, then turn them on edge and resaw them in half with a table saw or band saw. Done carefully with a jig, this results in two strips just less than $\frac{3}{8}$ inch thick, each with one good planed side. For fancier installations, both sides can be planed, sanded, and sometimes matched for color and grain. Finished bright with a light color wood like fir, spruce, or pine, the strips do a lot to brighten and enhance a dark or bare hull. Carefully fit the strip ends against bulkheads, or cut to a pleasing oval shape and router the edges with a $\frac{1}{8}$-inch or $\frac{1}{4}$-inch bullnose round. We attach the strips with flathead screws sunk flush or with screw caps. On

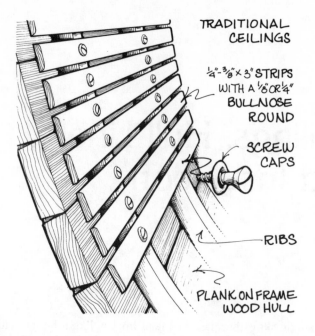

TRADITIONAL CEILINGS

¼"-⅜" × 3" STRIPS WITH A ⅛" OR ¼" BULLNOSE ROUND

SCREW CAPS

RIBS

PLANK ON FRAME WOOD HULL

large boats with thick ceiling strips, we plug the countersunk screw holes. Such ceilings provide a comfortable, form-fitting backrest against the hull and also shield the hull sides from damage by heavy gear stowed down in the bilge or up in the forepeak. Fitted on the overhead, they protect your head from protruding deck beams. Unlike a sealed tongue-and-groove overhead, they allow easy inspection of hardware fittings and the hull-to-deck joint. And, if attached with screws, the strips are easily removed for repair, refinishing, or to attach hardware to the hull or deck. Furthermore, this arrangement looks nautical and encourages thorough circulation of air, so vital to the long-term health of plank-on-frame hulls.

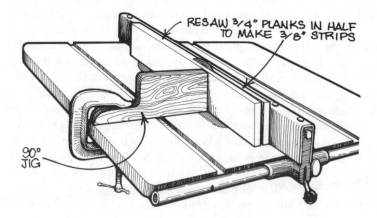

RESAW ¾" PLANKS IN HALF TO MAKE ⅜" STRIPS

90° JIG

The strips add minimal strength (at least the way they are usually built), although they can stiffen smaller hulls considerably if you use large fastenings that screw into frames.

For insulation, sheets of foam can be fitted and slipped into place behind the strips and still be easily removed for hull inspection or hardware placement. For appearance's sake, you might want to cover the foam sheets with fabric. Above the waterline on planked hulls, the strips could be glued onto structural foam, such as contoured Airex or Klegecell. The result will be a ceiling that contributes considerably to hull stiffness and insulation that is long wearing and good looking. Considering the limited number of insulation options available with plank-on-frame hulls because of the ever-present moisture problem, these methods are among the most viable.

Beam-and-Panel Ceilings

If your boat has interior deck beams, you can use them to tailor an attractive and easy-to-build beam-and-panel ceiling. The panels are held in place by removable ⅜-inch-thick trim strips, which are screwed into the beams and overlap each side of the beam by ½ inch. Under each panel, between the beams, go sheets of insulating foam. This simple system allows relatively easy access to the deck for attaching hardware and inspection. The panels can be made of anything that improves the look of the interior, including oiled hardwood plywood, painted plywood, fabric-covered panels, or even textured rice paper glued to thin plywood. The insulation should fit tightly between the panel and underside of the deck.

Veneer Hull Liners

One-eighth-inch thick wood veneer is perfect for stiffening, insulating, and sound-deadening a hull and is an attractive way to dress up the interior of a cold-molded, fiberglass, or metal hull. When epoxy-glued directly to the hull sides, it will bend easily to a fairly tight radius, such as is often found on bilge and hull curves in small boats.

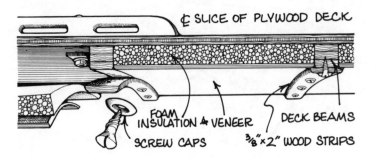

¢ SLICE OF PLYWOOD DECK

FOAM INSULATION & VENEER   DECK BEAMS

SCREW CAPS   ⅜"×2" WOOD STRIPS

The superior tenacity of epoxy makes this treatment possible in glass hull interiors. The advantage for the do-it-yourselfer is that the work may be done a small section at a time. Once glued in place, the veneer is there to stay and looks exactly like a cold-molded interior.

The main difficulty is holding the veneer firmly against the hull until the epoxy kicks. For bracing, clamps and plenty of long boards that can reach the other side of the hull allow an infinite variety of adjustments. Use a flexible pad to spread the clamping force over a larger area and to protect the veneer surface. Wedges may also be helpful to adjust the clamping pressure. Along edges and in corners not covered by the braces, short staples will sometimes penetrate a glass hull matrix just far enough to provide holding power. Use caution to prevent stapling through a thin glass hull.

To apply wood veneer to a fiberglass hull, the section where the veneer is to be glued should be as smooth as possible. Avoid sanding the hull unless it is very rough from sloppy workmanship and has lots of fine, stiff hairs of fiberglass that stick up. Wash the area with soap and water or solvent to remove wax. When the surface is dry, trowel epoxy resin thickened with a 50-50 mixture of silica and red microballoons onto the hull with a wide putty knife. Be sure the mixture covers the surface. In addition, apply a coating of unthickened epoxy resin to the side of the wood veneer to be glued. Now bend the veneer into place and carefully shore and brace it with the clamps and boards. If it's a long piece of veneer with considerable shape, try to arrange all the braces beforehand and have them ready to snap into place. Short, narrow strips will be much easier to apply than long, wide strips. *Caution: Braces and wedges can exert tremendous force, so exercise care that you do not push the hull "out of fair." Any bulge or unfairness you put into the hull may remain after the*

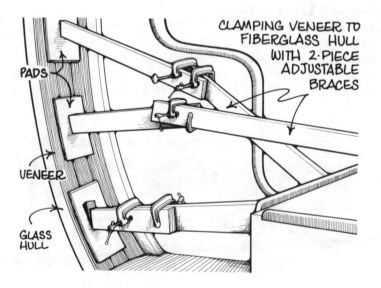

CLAMPING VENEER TO
FIBERGLASS HULL
WITH 2-PIECE
ADJUSTABLE
BRACES

PADS

VENEER

GLASS
HULL

braces are removed because of the added stiffness of the veneer and hardened epoxy.

Wipe off any excess epoxy from around the edges. Once the epoxy is dry, scrape or sand down to bare wood before finishing. The veneer surface may be sealed with three coats of clear epoxy resin or oiled or varnished. Additional laminations can easily be added by fastening them to the first layer with staples (which are removed after the epoxy kicks). As always when working with epoxy, take care to observe recommended safety precautions and provide plenty of ventilation.

The same veneer treatment can be used on aluminum hulls, but in addition to cleaning, a good sanding or acid-etch treatment is required for the best bonding. Epoxy suppliers can supply information and etching solutions for preparing aluminum surfaces.

Plywood Grates

Wood grates dress up plain, uninteresting decks, galleys, and heads while providing a positive non-skid surface that keeps feet a bit drier. Grates may also add stiffness to a sole or deck, as long as there are sufficient channels underneath to route water overboard or to a drain.

Traditional grates usually are made of teak or other suitable weather- and water-resistant hardwood ripped into strips and notched to half lap together. Traditional timber gratings are good looking when skillfully built, but require a table saw, a dado blade of some type, and exacting assembly. Without an effective, longlasting, waterproof glue they may require fastenings at every crossover to hold the separate strips together, and they work only in a completely flat area. Besides, even the best built timber grates can warp, split, and gradually decay when left without regular maintenance.

Most of these problems can be solved by using top-quality hardwood plywood instead of timber. The best available brands wear as well or better than timber, are available in various hardwood overlays, are dimensionally stronger than timber grates, and last better than solid timber. Plywood grates are also easier to build and finish than traditional timber grates. A router guided by a straightedge or jig will easily cut grate holes to any shape desired. Thinner plywood grates will also conform to curved decks and cambered cockpits, whereas timber grates won't.

The thickness and type of plywood appropriate for grates depends on the intended location. A cockpit will require thicker plywood to keep the feet dry, but a grate for the interior sole or shower may need to be only $\frac{1}{4}$ inch thick. On deck, teak-faced plywood might be best to match the teak trim around the cockpit. Light-colored ply-

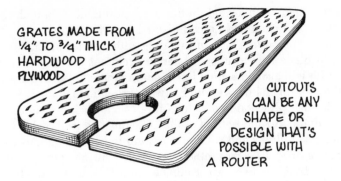

GRATES MADE FROM ¼" TO ¾" THICK HARDWOOD PLYWOOD

CUTOUTS CAN BE ANY SHAPE OR DESIGN THAT'S POSSIBLE WITH A ROUTER

wood grates can brighten a small, cramped interior and make it seem larger.

The hole design for a plywood grate can be a regular pattern of squares or diamonds, circles, ovals, or a custom logo to match the boat. Whatever the design, it should be planned with bare feet in mind. Widely spaced holes larger than ¾ inches in diameter or with sharp edges will not be comfortable. Before cutting into a large sheet, first make a small test piece and stand on it in your own bare feet.

A router with carbide cutter bit is the easiest and most efficient way to cut the pattern of holes in the grating. Depending on the desired pattern, a pair of long straightedges clamped across the grate may be sufficient to control the router, but if you have trouble free-handing the router—and it can be tricky if you're not used to it—it's safer to use a jig of some sort. Rounds or more complex designs require a jig or pattern board. (For more on handling a router, refer to Part I, pages 11–14.)

After the holes are cut into the grate, hand sand the top edges,

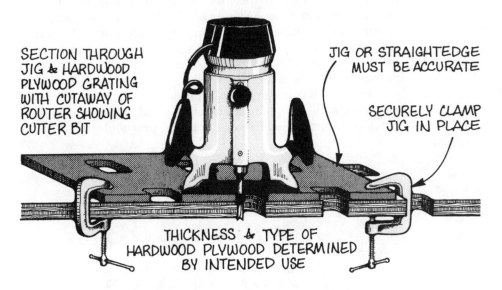

SECTION THROUGH JIG & HARDWOOD PLYWOOD GRATING WITH CUTAWAY OF ROUTER SHOWING CUTTER BIT

JIG OR STRAIGHTEDGE MUST BE ACCURATE

SECURELY CLAMP JIG IN PLACE

THICKNESS & TYPE OF HARDWOOD PLYWOOD DETERMINED BY INTENDED USE

or radius them with a small bullnose rounding bit. A ⅛-inch radius is usually sufficient and helps finish stick to the edge.

Score the bottom side of the grate with a series of shallow saw or dado blade cuts to allow water to drain easily away. A groove router bit will also do a good job of cutting these holes. We normally cut these drain channels about halfway through the grate: ⅛ inch for ¼-inch-thick plywood and ⅜ inch for ¾-inch-thick plywood.

Both the top and bottom of the grate must be well sealed to protect against mildew and rot. For a natural finish, the options are oil, varnish, a two-part clear urethane, or, best of all, an epoxy resin soak followed by clear two-part urethane paint. The epoxy treatment is labor intensive and expensive, but it will wear ruggedly and retain the natural look for five years or more. Properly applied, epoxy also protects the inner plywood laminations.

Paint will provide the maximum protection from sunlight and if applied over an epoxy seal will last for many years. Painting grates can be time consuming, because you must pay particular attention to the edges of plywood and each of the holes that form the pattern. If the grate is not too large, try wrapping it in a large plastic bag and fill the bag with enough paint to cover the grate. It's a messy operation at best, but it does a good job of soaking all the edge grain of the plywood. Varnish and epoxy applications require a brush and small roller. Hang the grate to dry instead of leaving it on a flat surface, where excess finish may form drops on the underside and in the pattern holes.

If additional non-skid is desired, non-skid paint or washed sand sprinkled into wet paint or epoxy may be applied over the plywood. When using sand, the trick is to stay off the grate for as long as a week to let the surface harden, then wash the excess sand off with a hose, let dry, and apply a couple of additional coats of paint. This will produce an aggressive non-skid that will last through years of hard wear, and that can be painted over at any time to renew the surface. This type of non-skid is best for use on deck; it's too rough for comfortable use below decks.

Often grates are simply fitted and laid in place, but if there is any danger of their slipping around, they should be screwed in place with bronze or stainless screws. For added structural reinforcement,

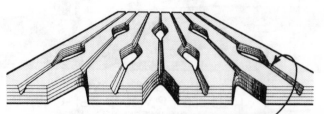

UNDERSIDE OF GRATE SCORED WITH A V-GROOVE ROUTER BIT TO ALLOW WATER TO DRAIN

PLASTIC WASHERS CAN BE
USED ON UNDERSIDE OF GRATE FOR DRAINAGE

they can also be epoxy glued in place, but then they can't be easily removed for cleaning underneath.

Another way to provide drainage, promote faster drying and longer grate life, and put a slight bounce to your step, is to screw plastic washers or attach wood or rubber cleats under the grate. Rubber cleats also prevent the grate from slipping.

Interior Lockers, Bins, and Compartments

All boats benefit from an abundance of watertight storage spaces to keep contents organized and dry. On small boats, these compartments can also stiffen the hull and provide additional flotation. Integral compartments tightly sealed inside and out with epoxy resin are easy to build into fiberglass and cold-molded hulls; epoxy fillets are all it takes to hold the units in place. In plank-on-frame hulls, modular compartment units should be assembled first, then fastened—either temporarily or permanently—to ribs or bulkheads.

Design Considerations

Designing storage spaces in small, crowded hulls takes considerable experimentation and forethought. The compartments should be planned around what will be placed in them, especially if the items are large or have an unusual shape. For long and bulky items that might have to be carried on deck, such as an extra pair of oars, an extra boothook, or maybe even an inflatable raft, the large spaces under the berths are ideal. You will have to provide access hatches of appropriate size, plus the room to maneuver the pieces in and out. Do some dry runs with the actual items that will be stored in each space. I once built a special underberth compartment that was made to hold a pair of spruce spoon oars for a racing shell. With its specially shaped hatchcovers it turned out very nicely—until I realized that the oars were too long to be maneuvered into the cabin and inside the compartment.

As discussed in Part III, watertight compartments can provide considerable flotation potential. To maximize their potential, try to locate access ports or hatches on top instead of on the sides, and seal

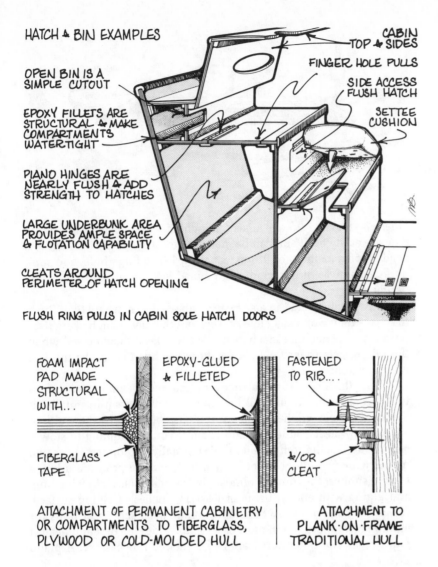

HATCH & BIN EXAMPLES

CABIN TOP & SIDES

FINGER HOLE PULLS

OPEN BIN IS A SIMPLE CUTOUT

SIDE ACCESS FLUSH HATCH

SETTEE CUSHION

EPOXY FILLETS ARE STRUCTURAL & MAKE COMPARTMENTS WATERTIGHT

PIANO HINGES ARE NEARLY FLUSH & ADD STRENGTH TO HATCHES

LARGE UNDERBUNK AREA PROVIDES AMPLE SPACE & FLOTATION CAPABILITY

CLEATS AROUND PERIMETER OF HATCH OPENING

FLUSH RING PULLS IN CABIN SOLE HATCH DOORS

FOAM IMPACT PAD MADE STRUCTURAL WITH...

EPOXY-GLUED & FILLETED

FASTENED TO RIB....

FIBERGLASS TAPE

&/OR CLEAT

ATTACHMENT OF PERMANENT CABINETRY OR COMPARTMENTS TO FIBERGLASS, PLYWOOD OR COLD-MOLDED HULL

ATTACHMENT TO PLANK·ON·FRAME TRADITIONAL HULL

the top or extend it well above the waterline. Remember that a partially flooded hull will be lower in the water than usual and compartments with unsealed tops near the waterline will fill with water. Gasketed tops or tight-fitting hatchcovers will suffice, but the best way to seal a compartment and provide fast access is with the small, screw-in hatches described in Part III. While these are available only in smaller sizes that may restrict the types of items that can be stowed, they do a credible job of sealing with a minimum of building work.

Flush-Fitting Hatchcovers

Flush-fitting hatchcovers fit easily under cushions on settees or bunks, and in various nooks and crannies to provide entrance to

FOR ROUNDED HATCHES PLYWOOD SUPPORTS
ARE EASY TO CUT TO UNUSUAL SHAPES
& STRONGER THAN
TIMBER CLEATS

otherwise isolated storage areas. Though difficult to make watertight, they are easily built and can be made in any size and shape. All they need is some method for lifting, usually a 1-inch fingerhole, and support cleats of sawn plywood epoxy glued in place around the hatch perimeter.

These hatchcovers can also be used above decks, where their flush fit means they won't snag toes, sheets, or other gear. But be sure they have a secure latching mechanism that will keep them closed when the sailing gets rough. A lightweight tether line tied to the top is a wise precaution.

Once the flush-fitting hatchcover is marked, it should be cut carefully because the cutout will become the cover. Keep in mind that the marked hole will be smaller around its perimeter by the width of the support cleats, so leave extra room if you're planning to stow a specific item in the compartment. We normally cut support cleats two inches wide and allow about ⅜ inch or ½ inch to protrude into the hole to support the top. We almost always attach cleats by clamping and gluing with epoxy, using at least 1½ inches of gluing surface. Cleats for large or heavy hatchcovers may need screws or bolts for additional support, but in most cases epoxy does the best and neatest job. Hinges and other hardware can be added if necessary. A piano

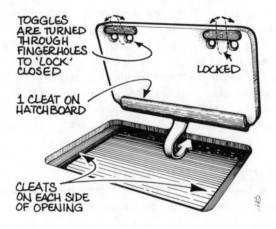

TOGGLES
ARE TURNED
THROUGH
FINGERHOLES
TO 'LOCK'
CLOSED

LOCKED

1 CLEAT ON
HATCHBOARD

CLEATS
ON EACH SIDE
OF OPENING

hinge, preferably bronze or stainless steel, is the strongest. If it must be flush, you will need to remove about ¼ inch of wood from under the hinge with a paring chisel and small rabbet plane.

Small toggles of hardwood attached to the underside of the hatch-cover will make a flush-fitting hatchcover self-locking. Flipped open or closed through one or two fingerholes, the toggles are held in place with a small machine screw or bolt with a plastic-lined antivibration nut on the end to keep it from falling off. Some fine tuning may be necessary to get the toggles working just right; wax or a slight bevel on the ends may help. If the toggles become loose with age or use, take another turn on the nuts.

Bins

Bins are very simple compartments, often without doors or covers, and are very helpful in organizing gear and supplies aboard a small boat. I like small groups of open-front or low-front bins for all the things I often need close at hand, but which need a permanent home. I can see instantly what I want, and the retaining front keeps every-thing in place. These pigeonhole units can be built against the hull or against a bulkhead and can be either modular or structural. If filleted to the hull, bin sides can also serve as hull stiffeners.

Drop-out bins are large, triangular-shaped compartments, some-times called "galley bins" because they are ideally suited for pots and pans, 25-pound bags of potatoes or rice, and other large, heavy pieces that always seem in the way. Their triangular shape keeps items from rattling around as they might in a flat-bottomed compartment. And the more heavily a bin is loaded, the more stable it becomes.

Bins work best down near the sole, where they can be fitted right against the hull, making use of what is otherwise an odd-shaped

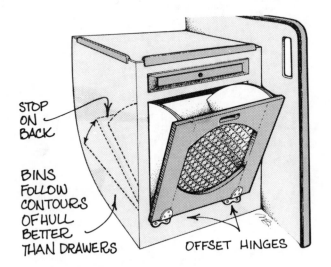

STOP ON BACK

BINS FOLLOW CONTOURS OF HULL BETTER THAN DRAWERS

OFFSET HINGES

space. All they require is a couple of hinges and a latching mechanism of some type. For ventilation, the front can be caned; you can also cut small vent holes in the sides of the bins. Galley bins should be as large as possible, with considerable depth to provide a counterweight to keep them closed. If they must be made shallow because of space restrictions, rig a shock cord to hold them closed.

Plywood/Epoxy Water and Storage Tanks

We've often needed extra tank space in our boats. Over the years, we experimented with a wide variety of portable tanks but found none really satisfactory. Metal cans left rust rings on everything they touched, and ruined the teak gratings we built to keep them off the bottoms of the lockers. Plastic tanks, even the best we could find, lost their shape and sometimes split without warning after exposure to sunlight. Galvanized, stainless steel, fiberglass, and rubber sausage tanks had certain advantages, but none offered the range of features we wanted, including low cost and ease of customizing.

A far more satisfactory alternative is to make your own tanks out of hardwood plywood, fiberglass cloth, and epoxy. They are easily built to any size or shape, and they offer many other advantages as well. In most cases, plywood tanks are lighter than other types and can be easily customized—baffled, vented, or drained as needed, and made thin-walled or thick-walled to suit the application. There are no electrolysis problems, and all the plumbing can be plastic, and installed with simple woodworking tools. Moreover, once scrubbed and rinsed they have less aftertaste than any other type of tank we've ever used.

The usefulness of these tanks is limited only by your imagination. We've built galley top or cabinet tanks for gravity flow to the sink, and we've installed tanks in unused areas of the bilge. We've also built large, deck-mounted tanks that are easily filled from dockside and provide gravity flow to anywhere in the boat. These water tanks may also be used for other types of storage such as food, supplies, and even gear. Sealed, they provide an extra measure of positive flotation should the hull spring a leak.

Further illustrating the adaptability of plywood tanks, we once

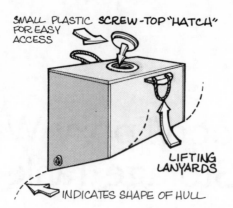

SMALL PLASTIC **SCREW-TOP "HATCH"** FOR EASY ACCESS

LIFTING LANYARDS

INDICATES SHAPE OF HULL

made a tall, narrow tank that fitted against the backside of a hanging locker, supported on hooks. We have also made portable tanks with built-in carrying handles. One tank was specifically fitted to a flat space in a small dinghy, which made trips ashore to refill much easier. Removable tanks are a welcome convenience when living at anchor or on a mooring, as long as they can be easily loaded and unloaded.

Construction Techniques

We usually construct tanks with scrap pieces of plywood, small odd-shaped bits that are good for little else. Smaller, 5- and 10-gallon water tanks can be built of thin plywood (1/8 inch and up) epoxy sealed and sheathed with glass cloth. Most of our tanks are built from 1/4-inch-thick plywood, although for 30- to 40-gallon water tanks we've used 3/4-inch plywood with substantial internal reinforcement.

All tanks are usually sheathed inside and out with 6-ounce fiberglass cloth saturated with epoxy. It's not always necessary to sheathe quality hardwood plywood, but domestic marine plywood must be sheathed to prevent hairline cracks. Normally we sheathe the plywood pieces separately before the tank is assembled. In larger tanks, we also use corner posts for extra support, and put fillets on every inside corner to prevent sharp crevices that might harbor bac-

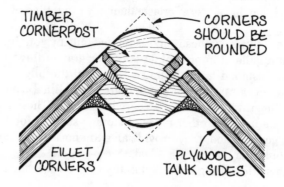

TIMBER CORNERPOST

CORNERS SHOULD BE ROUNDED

FILLET CORNERS

PLYWOOD TANK SIDES

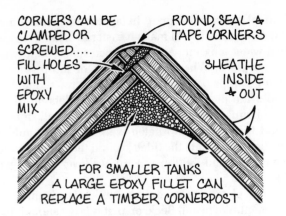

CORNERS CAN BE CLAMPED OR SCREWED..... FILL HOLES WITH EPOXY MIX

ROUND, SEAL & TAPE CORNERS

SHEATHE INSIDE & OUT

FOR SMALLER TANKS A LARGE EPOXY FILLET CAN REPLACE A TIMBER CORNERPOST

teria or be hard to clean. Sharp corners are susceptible to breaks through the epoxy seal, so we round the edges inside and outside the tank with a block plane to help the epoxy stick better. Although we always use corner posts on large tanks for the added strength, most water tanks can be built without them. We simply fillet the inside corners with a large radius and reinforce the outside corners with an additional layer of fiberglass tape.

Most tanks, especially the smaller sizes, are built without fastenings of any kind, but if fastenings are used, they should all be silicone bronze screws countersunk and sealed with a mixture of epoxy and microballoons. All interior and exterior surfaces not sheathed with glass cloth are rolled or brushed with no fewer than three coats of epoxy resin. Pay particular attention to plywood edges, rolling extra coats to ensure a long-term seal. We also apply a couple of coats of epoxy resin to all interior fillets; this makes a slick, shiny surface that is easier to keep clean. Tanks exposed to sunlight on a regular basis, such as deck-mounted gravity flow tanks, need an exterior coat of paint.

Large, flat tanks probably will need internal baffles to dampen sloshing—otherwise, you may lie in your bunk at night listening to water gurgling in the tanks. Baffles filleted to the tank sides will pro-

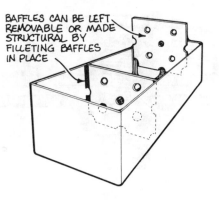

BAFFLES CAN BE LEFT REMOVABLE OR MADE STRUCTURAL BY FILLETING BAFFLES IN PLACE

vide additional structural support in larger tanks, but removable baffles fitted between cleats will make it easier to clean or inspect a tank.

To fit a water tank into an odd-shaped space, simply fit one side at a time into place. When you have two or more sides in correct position with clamps or temporary nails or screws, attach small tack fillets to hold the pieces in place. After the fillets harden, carefully remove the clamps and complete the fillet. When all sides are tacked together and the interior is filleted well enough to hold its shape, remove the tank, complete the fillets, round the outside edges slightly with block plane, sand lightly, and apply a layer of fiberglass tape to the outside corners.

Inspection plates are necessary for repair, cleaning, and hardware attachment. We install Beckson plates large enough to fit a hand through, and located so that you can reach into any corner of the tank for cleaning or plumbing. These deck plates are easy to install and are available in clear acrylic to permit interior inspection of the tank and its contents.

Drain, fill, and vent plumbing, if required, will vary from simple to sophisticated according to the situation and individual taste. The simplest tanks contain only a fill on the top, perhaps just a screw-in deck plate. Tanks can be hooked to other tanks with hoses and shut-off valves, and plastic plumbing can be routed from tank to galley or head in just about any configuration desired.

For tanks that drain from the bottom, the drain can be elevated slightly above the bottom of the tank to allow sediment to settle where it can be cleaned out. Other situations may require an emptying drain that leaves nothing inside the tank. For these emptying drains (and shower stalls), we fit a piece of ¾-inch-thick plywood to the bottom of the tank, mark and cut the piece from each corner to the drain location, then take the separate pie-shaped pieces and plane them to a wedge shape, so that each piece slopes downhill toward the drain. Reinstalled using epoxy glue to seal all surfaces, it makes a bottom that will dry completely when empty.

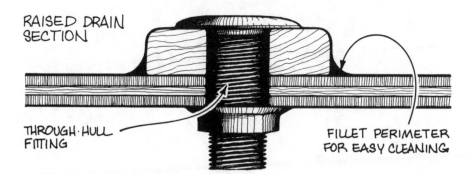

RAISED DRAIN
SECTION

THROUGH·HULL
FITTING

FILLET PERIMETER
FOR EASY CLEANING

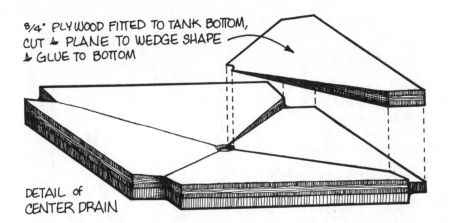

3/4" PLYWOOD FITTED TO TANK BOTTOM,
CUT & PLANE TO WEDGE SHAPE
& GLUE TO BOTTOM

DETAIL of
CENTER DRAIN

Plywood/Epoxy Sinks

A properly designed sink of the right size for your boat will add a
lot to the convenience of handling fresh water. After some 10 years
of searching the marketplace for sturdily built and well-designed boat
sinks, we now build our own sinks of plywood and epoxy, which
allows them to be custom-fitted to exact sizes and depths. Plywood
sinks also keep hot water hot longer because of their superior insulating value, and if well built and trimmed out with a nice teak molding they are quite good looking. They can also be painted to match
the galley trim.

To construct a plywood/epoxy sink, follow the basic instructions
for building plywood/epoxy tanks, described earlier in this section.
We build our sinks out of hardwood plywood, ¼ inch thick for small,
lightweight sinks and as thick as 1 inch for larger sinks that can benefit
from the insulating value of the thicker wood. The sink can be square
or rectangular to match available counter or undercounter space. Its
sides can be either straight or tapered, and you can even design a
double sink if you need the extra space. Make the sink as deep as

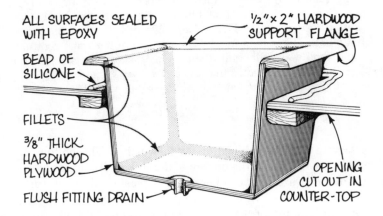

ALL SURFACES SEALED
WITH EPOXY

½"x 2" HARDWOOD
SUPPORT FLANGE

BEAD OF
SILICONE

FILLETS

3/8" THICK
HARDWOOD
PLYWOOD

FLUSH FITTING DRAIN

OPENING
CUT OUT IN
COUNTER-TOP

No-Frills Water Storage Systems for Small Boats

Small boats do not always lend themselves to conventional methods of fresh water storage and dispensing. There is often not sufficient room in the small hull for the complex system of tankage, pumps, and pipe to route water on demand from tank to sink. But there are alternatives, some of them actually superior in some ways to more complicated, expensive, and time-consuming systems. When designing and building a water system for the small boat the words of Thoreau may be most useful—"Simplify, simplify!"

2½ TO 5 GALLON PLASTIC JUGS WITH SPIGOTS ARE SIMPLE

Although the water system needs of our clients have been diverse, from one-gallon jugs in the bilge to hot tubs, for our own series of small boats we usually design a no-frills system. Smaller boats seem to get by very well with five- or ten-gallon "master" tanks, from which one-gallon jugs and the sink are filled as needed. A slightly larger boat might get along very well with modular bilge tanks equipped with manual or even 12-volt electric pumps that deliver water to the galley. Dishwater is then drained into an undersink container and emptied overboard, either manually or by a through-hull fitting situated above the waterline. (If the hull has a wide boottop stripe, this may be a good place to partially disguise the sink through-hull; it will leave only a small stain on the hull.) The advantage of an above-the-waterline drain is that if a fitting or connecting hose breaks, there is seldom a problem—unlike a below-the-waterline drain, which can flood the hull if it comes loose or leaks.

Gravity-flow tanks work well placed on deck, or below decks in overhead cabinets. They can be plumbed with PVC pipe and should always be equipped with positive shut-offs to avoid losing the whole waterworks by mistake.

A simple system for small boats is plastic tubing routed from the topside tank, with a positive shut-off at the source and a clothespin, or a tiny Jorgenson spring clamp, at the end.

The only disadvantage of gravity flow tanks, aside from the fact they are sometimes wasteful of water, is that they place the weight of all that water up high, instead of down low in the hull where it could improve stability. Fifteen or twenty gallons on deck can weigh as much as a person. In small boats I often rely on the weight of the water for additional ballast, and since five-gallon jugs are maneuverable, I usually try to store as many of them as possible down in the bilge. The five-gallon jugs can also be emptied as needed into the topside tank for controllable water management, or the jug can be equipped with an outlet cap of some type. One of the tidiest solutions for small hulls is to place five-gallon jugs under the sink, hook them to a foot pump, and pump the water right into the galley sink. This method also leaves your hands free and allows you to monitor precisely the amounts of water that are being used.

necessary to prevent spillage in rough weather. The bottom drain should be set flush with the bottom of the sink to drain properly, and the drain hardware can be either metal or plastic. All wood surfaces should be sealed with at least three coats of epoxy.

Around the top of the sink we fit a hardwood lip, usually with mitered corners, which supports the sink in the hole cut through the countertop. Either silicone or epoxy can be used to seal the sink into the countertop opening: Epoxy will make a more permanent fit, but silicone seal is best if you need to remove the sink later. For added convenience you might want to make a hardwood plug to fit over the top of the sink, to provide usable countertop space when the sink is not in use. And when you're underway, the sink can be used to stow coffee or tea cups, wrapped in a dishcloth.

Modular Cabinetry

Modular cabinetry and furniture are structures that can be built, installed, and if necessary, removed as a unit. Modular cabinetry is ideally suited for small boats, especially when modifying interior layouts to suit changing needs. A modular system is applicable to any type of hull construction: glass, metal, cold-molded, and plank-on-frame. Furthermore, a boat with a planned modular interior can be more easily emptied and made accessible for maintenance or repair, especially emergency repairs that have to be done in a hurry.

While modular compartments can be permanently secured to fiberglass and cold-molded hulls with epoxy fillets, bolts or screws allow each component to be easily removed. We once designed and equipped an 18-foot rowing dory with a completely modular interior. Furniture, thwarts, and sealed storage/flotation compartments were bolted to permanent plywood gussets. The gussets were epoxy glued to the hull sides and reinforced with large epoxy fillets. In addition to holding everything in place, the gussets furnished superb localized reinforcement to specific areas of the hull.

Any piece that can be built and prefinished "on the bench" will usually be much better built and more easily completed than if constructed "on location," amid the tangle of tools and materials inside the confines of a small, cramped hull. And if the finished component cannot fit through the hatch and into position in the hull, the module can be designed to come apart and reassemble inside the hull.

Patterning and Framing

When preparing to build a modular component, a mockup pattern made of individual plywood scraps scribed to the hull sides or deck

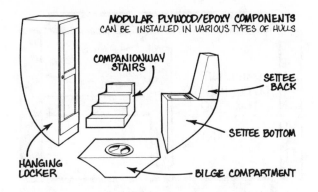

MODULAR PLYWOOD/EPOXY COMPONENTS
CAN BE INSTALLED IN VARIOUS TYPES OF HULLS

COMPANIONWAY STAIRS

SETTEE BACK

SETTEE BOTTOM

HANGING LOCKER

BILGE COMPARTMENT

and then clamped or stapled in place will help you determine the sizes and locations of details such as bins and doors (refer to the illustration on p. 18). Patterning is also often the easiest way to get a good fit inside a small, curvaceous hull. It may be possible to fit the actual plywood sides, back, front, and bottom right into the hull for scribing and marking and eliminate the patterning step, but only if there is adequate room below.

For most modular units, plywood is the best choice for the cabinet "box," or frame. If doors or drawers are required, adding a hardwood face frame to the front of the box will give the cabinetry a professional look and furnish an attachment point for door hinges. The face frame is added last, after the basic box is built and finished. If the plywood is ½ inch or thicker, it's easy to glue and screw the face frames right into the plywood edges, but thinner plywood usually requires small (¾-inch by ¾-inch) timber cleats for a better fastening surface. If possible, the cleats should be epoxy glued in place using clamps instead of fastenings. For a tight fit, the cleats should be flush with the edges of the box; trim them if necessary with a block plane after the glue cures.

We normally make the face frame ⅛ inch larger all around the perimeter, which eliminates some of the effort of making a perfect joint. We also always dowel face frame joints. Doweling takes a little extra time, but it is by far the strongest method. Using two hardwood dowel pins at each joint, we smear glue along the length of each pin,

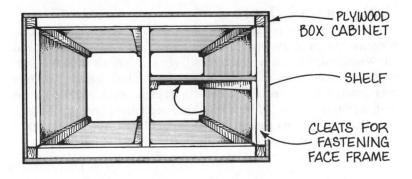

PLYWOOD BOX CABINET

SHELF

CLEATS FOR FASTENING FACE FRAME

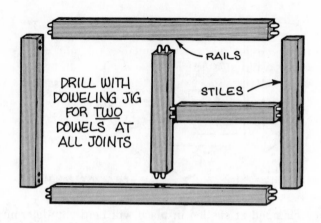

DRILL WITH DOWELING JIG FOR TWO DOWELS AT ALL JOINTS

RAILS

STILES

then insert them with a twisting motion. We also apply glue across the end grain of the rails (horizontal members) and stiles (vertical members). White glue is considered sufficient for most cabinetry, but epoxy glue will last a lot longer, won't crack, and is also best for boat cabinetry exposed to occasional weather or moisture.

Building face frames for cabinetry is something of an art. Professional builders often glue up the entire unit on a flat table, sand everything with a belt or orbital sander, and then install the completed unit on the boat. For first-timers, or for those building only a single module, it may be easier to construct the face frame components separately and attach them to each other right on the cabinet box. Gluing and clamping right on the box will ensure the proper clearances and fit all around. The only complication is that the face frame will have to be hand sanded after it is glued, in order to level and align the rails and stiles.

Attach the face frames to the plywood box with screws placed in carefully countersunk holes, and seal the screw holes with wood plugs made of the same wood as the face frames. Tapered drill bits equipped with adjustable countersinks are best for this operation, because the pilot hole for the screw and the countersink for the wood plug are done in one operation.

Drawers and Doors

Face frames can be designed to frame and support any combination of doors, bins, and drawers. Drawers are by far the most difficult and time-consuming to build, and unless there is a definite need for them we recommend bins, shelves, and regular cabinet doors. Installing the runners for drawers is what takes most of the work, but the drawer itself also takes considerable extra time, and unless properly built, it will stick or rattle in changing weather conditions. We used to build drawer runners of wood strips, sealed with epoxy and lubricated with beeswax, but now there are many types of prefabricated drawer sliders available that will provide a much smoother action with far less work.

Solid timber doors are beautiful, but they are notorious for warping and sticking and should be fitted very loose to allow them to shrink and swell. For most applications we prefer hollow-core or insert-panel doors. The frame of the door can be built of timber to match the face frames, while the center panel can be just about anything. Hardwood plywood makes very stable and attractive panels that will not warp as easily as solid timber. Hollow-core doors have two thin panels of plywood attached to the door frame; the space between can be left hollow or filled with insulation if desired. We have also made panels of Plexiglas, Lexan, mirrors, and fabric. Fabric facings glued to thin plywood panels quiet the often noisy interiors of small hulls, and the great variety of fabrics available provides a wide latitude of choice for every taste and decor. Painted panels brighten up the interior and provide a pleasing contrast if the timber frame of the door is finished bright.

For a classy door with good ventilation, we often install panels of pre-woven caning. Caned doors look very nice on small boats, are relatively easy to build, and are more rugged than they appear. Attaching the caning involves cutting a groove in the backside of the door frame with a router, then inserting the caning into the groove, along with a bamboo spline and some glue. Various types, sizes, and patterns of pre-woven caning are available from crafts suppliers, along with bamboo splines, specialty tools, and complete instructions. The process is easy even for a novice. Finish by applying a few coats of varnish or epoxy to the caning to make it more waterproof and to keep it from shrinking and swelling.

A door cut from ¾-inch-thick plywood with a ⅜-inch by ⅜-inch

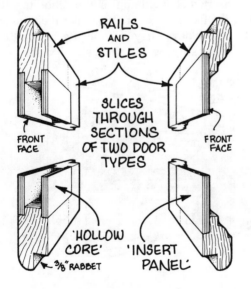

RAILS AND STILES

SLICES THROUGH SECTIONS OF TWO DOOR TYPES

FRONT FACE

FRONT FACE

'HOLLOW CORE'   'INSERT PANEL'

⅜" RABBET

rabbet in the backside avoids the need to build a frame of any kind. There is much to recommend an all-plywood door, especially on a boat, where moisture problems so inevitably will undermine well-fitted cabinetry, hatches, and doors. In contrast to timber, plywood is very stable dimensionally and looks great finished bright. Although it would probably be more expensive than using timber, you can build beautiful and unusual doors by cutting a one-piece frame from hardwood plywood and inserting a panel of any type. Another advantage to using hardwood plywood for one-piece door frames is that any design can be cut into it without splitting out the grain. Ovals, circles, anchor logos—just about anything is possible. Router details such as ogees, coves, or half rounds can be applied to the corners of hardwood plywood just like timber.

Hanging the Door

Doors can be fitted flush with the face frame or flat on top of the face frame, but the best solution is to fit the door halfway into the face frame, using standard brass ⅜-inch offset hinges set into a ⅜-inch by ⅜-inch rabbet cut on the backside edge of each door. Allow some slack on the top, bottom, and sides of the face frame opening so the door doesn't stick. As the offset hinges are installed, the backside rabbet may need an additional shaving with the rabbet plane to ensure proper clearance.

When attaching ⅜-inch offset hinges, first install both hinges on the door, measuring carefully to space them properly (tall, heavy doors may need three hinges). Then, positioning the door in the face frame opening, mark and drill a pair of pilot holes, using one hole on each hinge as a guide. Insert a screw in each hinge; then open and close the door. If additional adjustment is required, the other hinge screws can be inserted at slight angles to position the door perfectly in the center of the face frame opening. After the doors are installed on the boat for a few days, they may need a final fitting to remedy slight rubbing or sticking. A few shaves with a sharp rabbet plane

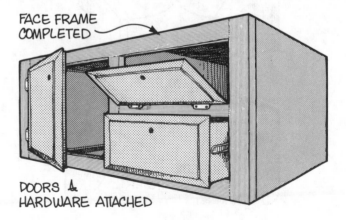

FACE FRAME COMPLETED

DOORS & HARDWARE ATTACHED

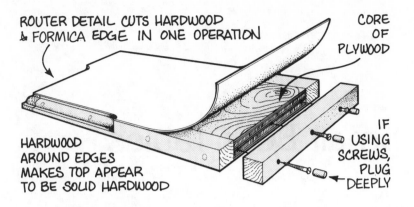

ROUTER DETAIL CUTS HARDWOOD & FORMICA EDGE IN ONE OPERATION

CORE OF PLYWOOD

HARDWOOD AROUND EDGES MAKES TOP APPEAR TO BE SOLID HARDWOOD

IF USING SCREWS, PLUG DEEPLY

are usually sufficient to do the job. All finishing should be done before the door is installed in the face frame.

Countertops

Though they are untraditional, plastic laminates such as Formica make fine, long-lasting countertops, moldings, and door panels. A great variety of colors and patterns is available, including simulated wood grains. Scraps of Formica from large countertops, chart tables, and galley surfaces can be used as matching panels for door frames. *Caution: The contact cement used to glue plastic laminates is toxic and flammable and should not be used below decks in a small boat without vigorous ventilation.*

To make a Formica countertop or tabletop appear to be affixed to a solid piece of hardwood, we epoxy-glue strips of hardwood to the edges of ¾-inch or 1-inch plywood. After planing and a light sanding to level all surfaces, we glue the sheet of Formica to the top. A router bit detail—ogee, cove, or bead pattern—is then cut into the hardwood and Formica edge in one operation, which leaves a very attractive edge. It's much easier and cheaper than building solid hardwood tables or counters, and without looking underneath it's hard to tell the difference.

Small Boat Tables

A well-designed table is a perpetually useful piece of furniture on a small boat, even if it must be folded away or stowed when not in use. Without a table of some sort, there isn't a convenient flat spot for books, charts, or a workbench, and meals end up being eaten from a deep bowl while you cradle a cup between your clenched feet.

A piece of plywood clamped across a thwart might do the trick under the boom tent at night, or you may have room for an articulated and infinitely adjustable banquet-sized spread. Once you begin to think in terms of space available, all sorts of options appear and you'll discover ideas and techniques to provide usable space in the tiniest of forepeaks or knee-bumping cockpits.

A small tray with a neck strap may be one of the simplest designs if you really have no room at all and need a surface on which to assemble your salad. Such trays are supremely adapted to small, lively hulls because you can balance continuously against the motion of the boat and keep a relatively level surface. It takes some experimenting, and spilling, to get just the right combination of strap length and body movements for a rolling boat. If it's really rough, you may need to tie the tray around your waist with shock cord.

We built a removable table for a small pram, stowed it under the thwart, and used it for years. It had a couple of bent brass hooks that fitted into inwale spaces and an adjustable leg on a hinge that supported it no matter where in the hull it was placed. By bending the brass hooks slightly, we could also make it work on other small dinghies and dories. It was great for a picnic afloat while drifting through the anchorage with the evening tide.

A keel-stepped mast or a mast support column, if appropriately located in the hull, offers another interesting option for supporting a

Portable Chart Table

For serious coastal navigating aboard a small boat, especially when singlehanding, it helps to have as many of the required navigation tools and instruments as possible in the cockpit or easily accessible from the cockpit. A permanent chart table below is fine (if the boat is large enough), but a small portable chart table will be much more useful in most circumstances.

Having the table in the cockpit saves running below to look at the chart, then back topside to check on your bearings. If properly fitted out, a cockpit chart table will keep the chart from being blown by the wind or soaked by an unexpected shower of spray. And, when navigating through winding channels or islands, the portable chart table can be turned to coincide with the compass reading.

A good grade ¼-inch or ⅜-inch plywood is probably the first choice for building the chart board. Hardboard (similar to the Masonite often used for clipboards) is a lightweight and workable alternative. With a plastic or wood molding around the edge, with spring clips fitted across the top and one side, and with a couple of extra clips to hold down the remaining two sides of the chart, you can have a relatively windproof, flat chart table that may be held in your lap or laid across the cockpit seats. Spring clips, both metal and plastic, are available in stationery

stores. Tablecloth clips are also handy and don't extend past the edge of the board.

The size of the board depends on the size of the charts you most often use. If you need a full, unfolded chart, be sure you have enough space to fit the board through the hatch and stow it below when not in use. If you always fold your charts, then a smaller size is possible and much more manageable. A folding board, using a plastic piano hinge, accommodates either full or folded charts and probably will be easy to stow.

A sheet of waterproof plastic will protect the chart from the weather and allow you to write and make notes without defacing the chart. Such a plastic piece, often found in art supply stores, can be held in place under the molding on one side of the plywood board or securely taped to the backside of the board along one edge. Stationery stores stock various types of pencils, pens, and inkmarkers that will write on almost anything. Take a scrap of the plastic sheeting into the store to find out which type works best. The marker should be water resistant, but you should be able to wipe the marks away easily with a soft towel. For night sailing, there are small, battery-powered, clip-on reading lights that furnish just the right size beam for reading details of the chart. A piece of red cellophane over the lamp will help preserve night vision.

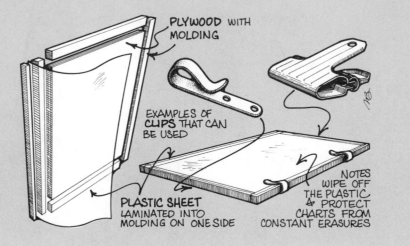

PLYWOOD WITH MOLDING

EXAMPLES OF CLIPS THAT CAN BE USED

PLASTIC SHEET LAMINATED INTO MOLDING ON ONE SIDE

NOTES WIPE OFF THE PLASTIC & PROTECT CHARTS FROM CONSTANT ERASURES

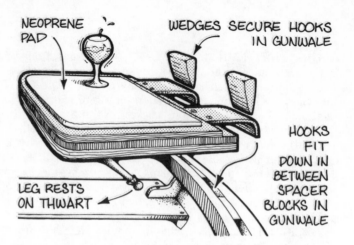

NEOPRENE PAD

WEDGES SECURE HOOKS IN GUNWALE

HOOKS FIT DOWN IN BETWEEN SPACER BLOCKS IN GUNWALE

LEG RESTS ON THWART ◄

table. The table shown in the illustration below is designed to slide up and down the mast. When not in use, it can be stored against the overhead, out of the way. Stops or supports hold it at the appropriate level when in use, and hooks hold it in place overhead. If the table is large and often leaned upon, adjustable support chains can be added to hold it in place. Small link brass chains are excellent table supports, and they stow easily and look good.

Tables supported by bulkheads vary from complex, accordion-leafed creations to simple, removable single- and double-leaf types. The simplest are supported by a cleat attached stoutly to the bulkhead with holes for dowels or pins to hold the table in place. A foldout leg or support chain is usually necessary unless the table can be sup-

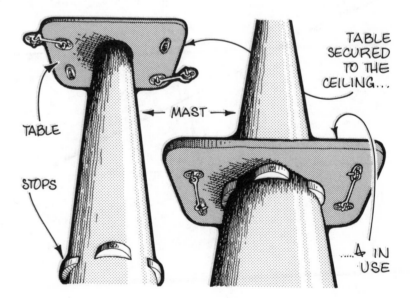

TABLE SECURED TO THE CEILING...

TABLE

← MAST →

STOPS

.....┵ IN USE

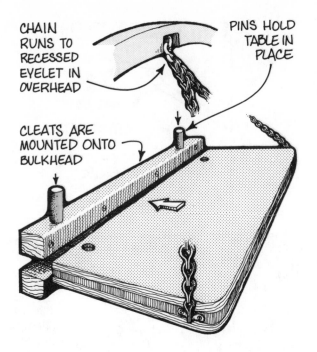

CHAIN RUNS TO RECESSED EYELET IN OVERHEAD

PINS HOLD TABLE IN PLACE

CLEATS ARE MOUNTED ONTO BULKHEAD

ported by a bunk or settee. When the table is removed and stowed, nothing is left except the cleat on the bulkhead.

Tables hinged to the bulkhead or hull can fold flush, up, or down, when not in use. The support can be a hinged knee that also folds flush and is held in place by a spot of Velcro. Piano hinges are always preferred since they provide maximum strength and good alignment along their entire length.

Centerboard trunks usually provide good support for a table, as long as the opened table doesn't restrict passage through the boat. If clearance is a problem, the table can often have separate folding leaves on either side or can be removable. Such tables are traditionally

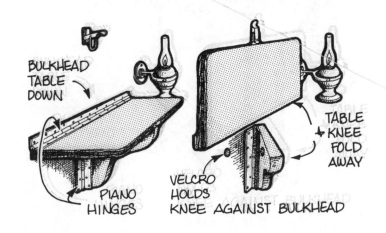

BULKHEAD TABLE DOWN

TABLE KNEE FOLD AWAY

PIANO HINGES

VELCRO HOLDS KNEE AGAINST BULKHEAD

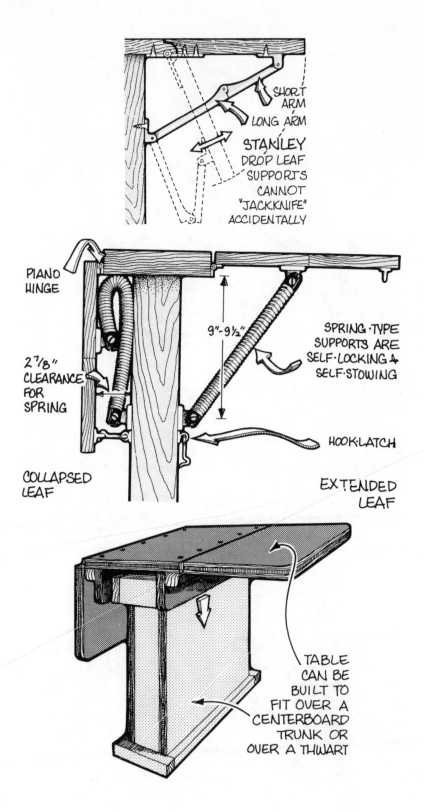

SHORT
ARM

LONG ARM

STANLEY
DROP-LEAF
SUPPORTS
CANNOT
"JACKKNIFE"
ACCIDENTALLY

PIANO
HINGE

9"-9½"

SPRING-TYPE
SUPPORTS ARE
SELF-LOCKING &
SELF-STOWING

2⅞"
CLEARANCE
FOR
SPRING

HOOK-LATCH

COLLAPSED
LEAF

EXTENDED
LEAF

TABLE
CAN BE
BUILT TO
FIT OVER A
CENTERBOARD
TRUNK OR
OVER A THWART

INTERIOR STOWAGE
AND CREATURE
COMFORTS

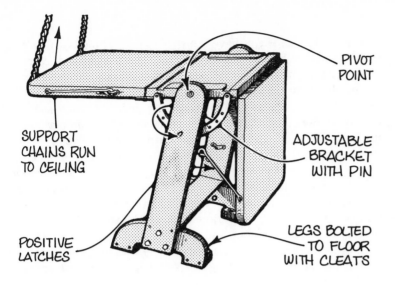

PIVOT POINT

SUPPORT CHAINS RUN TO CEILING

ADJUSTABLE BRACKET WITH PIN

POSITIVE LATCHES

LEGS BOLTED TO FLOOR WITH CLEATS

located fore and aft, but in small boats they may be mounted athwartships or whatever way works to best advantage.

For those long runs in the trades when the boat is on the same tack for days on end, a locking adjustable table is a big help in coping with the permanently inclined world below decks. The table, or a leaf of the table, can be held in position with a thumbscrew or adjustable bracket and set to accommodate the angle nearest to level.

A counterweighted drop-leaf table may be the ultimate in sea-

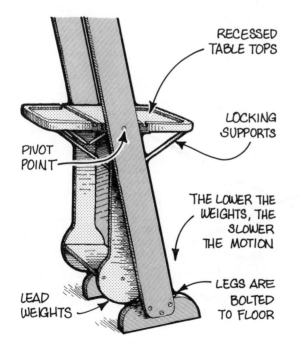

RECESSED TABLE TOPS

LOCKING SUPPORTS

PIVOT POINT

THE LOWER THE WEIGHTS, THE SLOWER THE MOTION

LEAD WEIGHTS

LEGS ARE BOLTED TO FLOOR

SMALL BOAT TABLES

153

going convenience if you have the space for it. Though it won't do much when the hull is nosediving into steep swells, a counterweighted table maintains a semblance of levelness athwartships. If nothing else, it makes a dandy conversation piece and your flatlander guests will talk endlessly about watching their sandwich sway up and down before them in response to every swell. The counterbalance must be well tuned. Too long or too short a counterweight arm, or too much or too little weight at the bottom will make the table either too sluggish or, at the other extreme, too snappy. Let a waterskier skim through a calm anchorage at dinner time, and an improperly balanced table will almost flip your dinner right into your lap. This tuning has to be done by experimentation because it will be different for every hull, displacement, and load. It is also a good idea to install a stop to lock the table in place at times. As with all large tables, the legs must be securely bolted to sole, bulkhead, or the ceiling.

Netting

Netting is a simple, yet effective means for making bunk bottoms, lifelines, and stowage containers, just to mention a few uses. Nets even catch fish. You can buy your nets, but it is difficult to find the right sizes and strengths needed for every purpose. The solution is to make your own nets to suit the uses you have in mind.

Netting materials are found in a number of styles and sizes in just about any marine supply store, and are also available by mail order. Sailmaker supply houses sometimes carry net making mate-

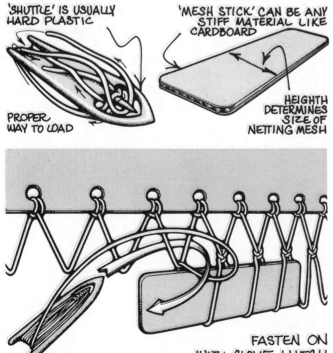

'SHUTTLE' IS USUALLY HARD PLASTIC

PROPER WAY TO LOAD

'MESH STICK' CAN BE ANY STIFF MATERIAL LIKE CARDBOARD

HEIGHTH DETERMINES SIZE OF NETTING MESH

FASTEN ON WITH CLOVE HITCH

· NETTING KNOT ·
BASIC SHEET BEND

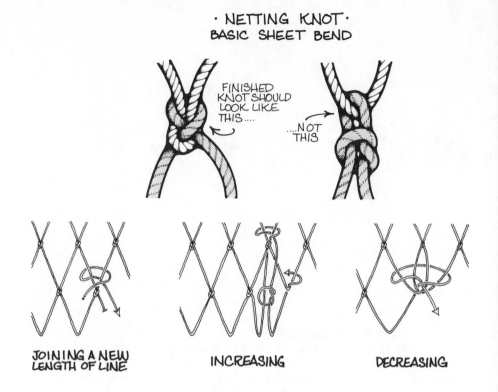

FINISHED KNOT SHOULD LOOK LIKE THIS....

....NOT THIS

JOINING A NEW LENGTH OF LINE

INCREASING

DECREASING

rials and tools. The mesh stick, used to gauge the size of the netting, may be cardboard, wood, or if you find a real antique, ivory. The mesh stick should be long enough to hold three mesh spaces at a time. Most shuttles are plastic and come in a number of sizes to accommodate materials ranging from fine string to ¼-inch braided line. The netting knot is a simple sheet bend and can be worked from left to right or right to left.

Experiment with different line and mesh sizes and materials, just to get an idea of what the finished product will look and feel like. A little practice is all it takes. Soon you'll have a net for everything from a hanging fruit basket to a full-size hammock for your 250-pound brother-in-law.

Part VI
Canvaswork

The Case for Canvas

The use of the word "canvas" to describe all fabric work on boats started centuries ago when bosuns made everything from sails to clothes out of canvas. The term is still used to mean anything aboard a boat made of fabric, even though very little of it today is actually made out of traditional cotton canvas.

Whatever the terminology, fabrics are particularly useful aboard small, lightweight craft with limited space and carrying capacity. Over the years, we've used fabric on our own boats in place of otherwise "solid" structures to cover, insulate, and cushion or increase stowage space, safety, and comfort. Fabric is often faster and easier to work with than plywood or timber or fiberglass, is less expensive and lighter, and can be more attractive. And compared to many boat-building jobs, working with fabric can be quite pleasant.

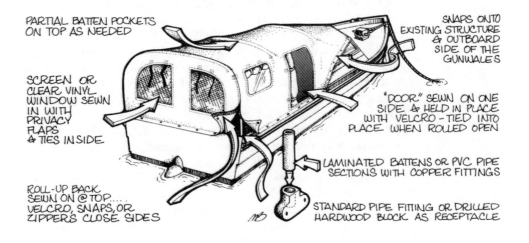

PARTIAL BATTEN POCKETS ON TOP AS NEEDED

SNAPS ONTO EXISTING STRUCTURE & OUTBOARD SIDE OF THE GUNWALES

SCREEN OR CLEAR VINYL WINDOW SEWN IN WITH PRIVACY FLAPS & TIES INSIDE

"DOOR" SEWN ON ONE SIDE & HELD IN PLACE WITH VELCRO - TIED INTO PLACE WHEN ROLLED OPEN

LAMINATED BATTENS OR PVC PIPE SECTIONS WITH COPPER FITTINGS

ROLL-UP BACK SEWN ON @ TOP..... VELCRO, SNAPS, OR ZIPPERS CLOSE SIDES

STANDARD PIPE FITTING OR DRILLED HARDWOOD BLOCK AS RECEPTACLE

Read's sailmaking sewing machine can be worked by one hand crank, or is adaptable to 110-volt or 12-volt current.

A sewing machine is handy for larger projects with yards of seams and hems, but we started doing canvaswork by hand and still make many small items that way. Our Read's hand crank sailmaking machine takes over when larger projects justify getting it out.

Find a good source for canvas. If you buy it in small quantities at the local marine supply store, you'll pay a premium, and you usually won't have a very wide choice. For years we've dealt with Seattle Fabrics, 3876 Bridge Way N., Seattle WA 98103. They provide a thick information package complete with samples that explain various types of fabrics and other valuable information. We always try to order in the largest quantities possible in order to get the best price. If you don't need very much and still want a good buy, try getting together a group order for roll quantities. We use a lot of brown, yellow, and tan, which seems to complement our natural wood hulls and spars, or you can go with the ever popular blue.

Canvas is now available in such a variety of weaves, blends, colors, and weights that the choices are almost unlimited. We've found the new acrylic fabrics to be virtually maintenance-free and so tough they seem to last forever. Treatments with a variety of sprays and paints render them virtually impervious to water, sunlight, and mildew. Fabric can be made moderately fire retardant for galley and other applications exposed to heat and can also be insulated with sewn-in layers of flexible foam or batting for colder climates. You can even order fabric with reflective foil backing if you wish to show up better on radar scopes.

As important as the fabric itself is the method of attachment. Besides the traditional grommet (see illustration on page 198), there is an astounding variety of fasteners and closures available for holding, stretching, lacing, supporting, and shaping a fabric structure. The choices include Velcro, studs, snaps and buttons, and zippers.

Insulated Covers

For winters aboard in the northwest and on high mountain lakes, we have made liberal use of batting and closed-cell insulating foam sewn between two pieces of fabric. Fitted over portholes, deck hatches, companionways, and bulkhead passageways, these cold weather covers keep the heat in, quiet the cabin, and add to privacy.

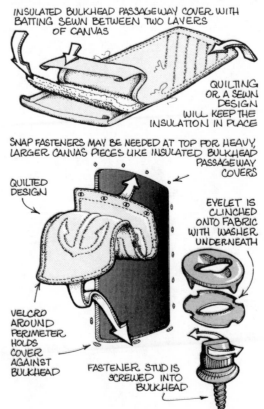

INSULATED BULKHEAD PASSAGEWAY COVER WITH BATTING SEWN BETWEEN TWO LAYERS OF CANVAS

QUILTING OR A SEWN DESIGN WILL KEEP THE INSULATION IN PLACE

SNAP FASTENERS MAY BE NEEDED AT TOP FOR HEAVY, LARGER CANVAS PIECES LIKE INSULATED BULKHEAD PASSAGEWAY COVERS

QUILTED DESIGN

EYELET IS CLINCHED ONTO FABRIC WITH WASHER UNDERNEATH

VELCRO AROUND PERIMETER HOLDS COVER AGAINST BULKHEAD

FASTENER STUD IS SCREWED INTO BULKHEAD

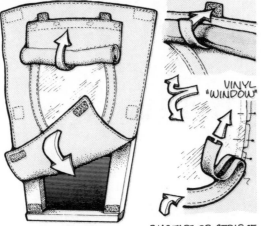

COMPANIONWAY COVER WITH VINYL "WINDOW" AND
"CURTAIN" SECURED WITH VELCRO

VINYL
"WINDOW"

BIAS TAPE OR STRIP OF
FABRIC CUT ON THE DIAGONAL

Unlike open-cell, or "sponge" foam, closed-cell foam doesn't absorb moisture, and will not readily absorb odors. It is available in thicknesses from ¼ inch to over ¾ inch, and even in thinner sheets, it adds sufficient stiffness to help hold itself in place. We usually attach the covers with spots or strips of Velcro and sometimes a permanent stud. Ties on one side or at the top hold the rolled piece in place when a passageway is opened.

Canvas companionway covers can be substituted for permanent wooden doors to shed wind, rain, and snow. We sew in a vinyl window for light below, and equip the window with a roll-down flap for privacy at night. This fabric "window" could also be constructed with netting to keep out bugs in the summertime. Fabric covers are a great first project to get used to working with fabric. If you're feeling creative, you can personalize them by sewing in your own design or adding an appliqué in a contrasting color or fabric to complement your interior.

Pipe Berths

Canvas pipe berths are very comfortable and add a sound-absorbing quiet to the inside of a hull. The bunk bottoms can be laced tight enough to satisfy a Marine Corps drill instructor, or loose enough to cradle the laziest sybarite. We once experimented successfully with hooked lengths of $\frac{5}{16}$-inch shock cord to provide more give. In hot weather, a canvas mattress is much cooler than other types, and in cold weather a thin, closed-cell foam pad or thicker lounge pad will keep the bunk cozy. The entire bunk bottom can be disassembled and folded away in a matter of minutes, or bagged for a trip to the laundromat. Quick release snaps or hooked sections of lace line assist quick removal. If the frame can be made "knockdown" or hinged, it will fold up against the hull to allow better use of a small boat's interior. For a complete "privacy pod" aboard a crowded boat, the bunk can be equipped with curtain and fabric compartments against the hull for insulation and personal stowage.

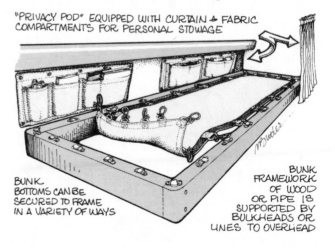

"PRIVACY POD" EQUIPPED WITH CURTAIN & FABRIC COMPARTMENTS FOR PERSONAL STOWAGE

BUNK BOTTOMS CAN BE SECURED TO FRAME IN A VARIETY OF WAYS

BUNK FRAMEWORK OF WOOD OR PIPE IS SUPPORTED BY BULKHEADS OR LINES TO OVERHEAD

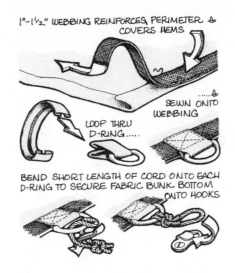

1"-1½" WEBBING REINFORCES PERIMETER & COVERS HEMS

LOOP THRU D-RING.....

.....& SEWN ONTO WEBBING

BEND SHORT LENGTH OF CORD ONTO EACH D-RING TO SECURE FABRIC BUNK BOTTOM ONTO HOOKS

Stout attachment points are always important, especially on such stressed pieces as bunk bottoms. A grommeting kit is well worth the money, but we've found that grommets usually need additional reinforcement. There are a variety of methods to reinforce attachment points, including double edges, webbing, and leather corner patches. We prefer to attach webbing around the perimeter of bunk bottoms, and to sew D-rings onto the webbing with doubled over fabric loops. With additional sewing, you can eliminate some or all of the hardware.

Futons

Futons are segmented folding cushions covered with a fabric and hinged to allow them to be folded into an unusual number of shapes and combinations. They are superb for large boats, but they fit nicely into the confines of small hulls because of their versatility. Futons make a perfect bunk mattress or a comfortable bed for the cockpit, forepeak, or deck—anywhere there is room to lay them out. Laid against the lifelines or cabin bulkhead, a futon makes a nice easy chair in the cockpit or cabin. Folded together, it stores in a small space; held together with a tie, it travels to and from the boat like a suitcase. Furthermore, futons can be easily custom built from inexpensive and readily available materials. Many expensive futons sold at furniture stores have a complicated adjustable wood frame of some sort, but the wood framework is an accessory, and the futon is entirely usable without any frame at all.

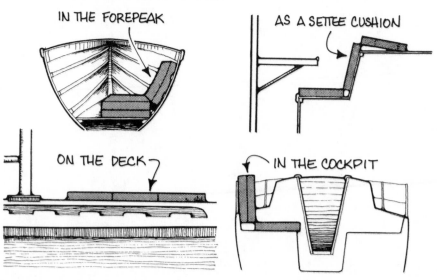

IN THE FOREPEAK

AS A SETTEE CUSHION

ON THE DECK

IN THE COCKPIT

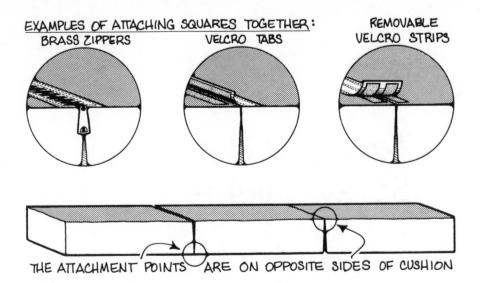

EXAMPLES OF ATTACHING SQUARES TOGETHER:

BRASS ZIPPERS   VELCRO TABS   REMOVABLE VELCRO STRIPS

THE ATTACHMENT POINTS ARE ON OPPOSITE SIDES OF CUSHION

The futon can be made thick or thin, from foam rubber or close-cell Ensolite pads. Our favorite for warm weather is a 2-inch-thick pad; for colder weather a thicker pad is warmer. The covering can be cotton for comfort or canvas for utility, and can be permanent or removable for easy washing. Use zippers, Velcro, lacing, or a combination of methods to attach the segments to one another.

Tents, Decking, and Spray Shields

Canvas decks, spray shields, and deck and cockpit tents can significantly increase your living space, make a rough passage a bit safer and dryer, and make sleeping aboard on a cold, wet night a pleasant experience. With proper support, structures made of fabric are comfortable, space saving, and lightweight, and with the addition of plastic windows, vent flaps, and mosquito netting, these structures can serve many needs.

Fabric structures used above decks should be as low as possible to keep windage to a minimum, and should employ good, heavier-weight fabric that doesn't stretch, fade, or wear quickly. Quality is related to price—you usually get what you pay for. Even shock cords may not be able to take up the slack of cheap fabric or wet, untreated canvas.

Support Systems

Like a good roof, fabric needs slope to shed moisture effectively; even a heavy dew will fill slack pockets in a flat or loose-fitting piece of fabric. No matter how well it's designed or what fabric is used, a structure that flaps, sags, or leaks is worse than none at all. A good support system is the key to success.

For a cockpit tent, a ridgepole is the simplest support. It usually runs fore and aft down the centerline, although it can be positioned on one side of a hull for a "lean-to" structure. A boom is the classic ridgepole, but we've also used a 10-foot sculling oar supported by a forward tripod and a notch in the transom. The disadvantage of a ridgepole system is that usable space in the tent is somewhat limited compared to the many other options for supporting fabric.

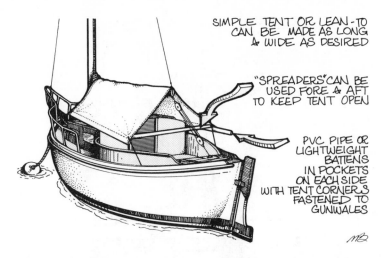

SIMPLE TENT OR LEAN-TO CAN BE MADE AS LONG & WIDE AS DESIRED

"SPREADERS" CAN BE USED FORE & AFT TO KEEP TENT OPEN

PVC PIPE OR LIGHTWEIGHT BATTENS IN POCKETS ON EACH SIDE WITH TENT CORNERS FASTENED TO GUNWALES

Halyards attached to sewn-in D rings can literally raise the roof on a cockpit tent, provided you are careful not to apply so much tension that you tear the whole affair off the hull and hoist it flapping to the masthead.

Interior telescoping supports, braced up from thwarts or the sole, are another option. I made three good supports from an old camera tripod. They adjust quickly to any length and can be stowed with ease. Fit the upper ends of these supports into a grommet or a reinforced patch on the fabric, or cushion the end with a punctured tennis ball.

Battens and Beams

Another method for supporting fabric is an external batten, rigged much like a mountain tent. Batten supports provide greater interior

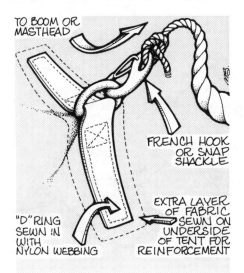

TO BOOM OR MASTHEAD

FRENCH HOOK OR SNAP SHACKLE

EXTRA LAYER OF FABRIC SEWN ON UNDERSIDE OF TENT FOR REINFORCEMENT

"D" RING SEWN IN WITH NYLON WEBBING

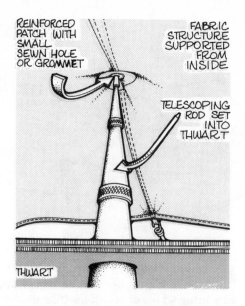

REINFORCED PATCH WITH SMALL SEWN HOLE OR GROMMET

FABRIC STRUCTURE SUPPORTED FROM INSIDE

TELESCOPING ROD SET INTO THWART

THWART

space than in a tent held up by a ridgepole, and there are no intrusions to dodge, as with telescoping supports. All you need to support an external batten system is a socket or shallow hole at the fore and aft ends to hold the batten, and small loops or ties along the rest of the batten length. If these ties are small-diameter shock cord, they can be adjusted to keep the fabric at exactly the correct tension to shed water and wind. Such a structure requires tie-downs only at corners and along the edges to be self-supporting, and after a session of fine tuning and adjusting the length of shock cords it should be relatively tough and trouble free.

Battens are also useful as interior support mechanisms, rigged

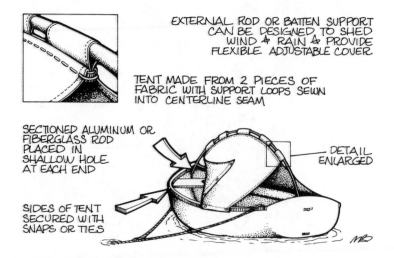

EXTERNAL ROD OR BATTEN SUPPORT CAN BE DESIGNED TO SHED WIND & RAIN & PROVIDE FLEXIBLE ADJUSTABLE COVER

TENT MADE FROM 2 PIECES OF FABRIC WITH SUPPORT LOOPS SEWN INTO CENTERLINE SEAM

SECTIONED ALUMINUM OR FIBERGLASS ROD PLACED IN SHALLOW HOLE AT EACH END

DETAIL ENLARGED

SIDES OF TENT SECURED WITH SNAPS OR TIES

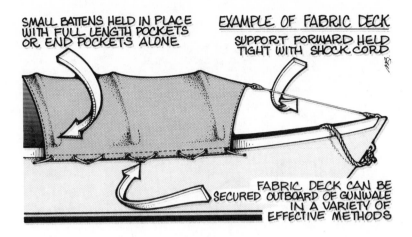

SMALL BATTENS HELD IN PLACE WITH FULL LENGTH POCKETS OR END POCKETS ALONE

EXAMPLE OF FABRIC DECK

SUPPORT FORWARD HELD TIGHT WITH SHOCK CORD

FABRIC DECK CAN BE SECURED OUTBOARD OF GUNWALE IN A VARIETY OF EFFECTIVE METHODS

under the fabric or between layers. Fabric decking can be supported by battens that fit into sockets or notches in the gunwale or deck, or by curved battens that fit into pockets in the fabric, as in the accompanying illustration.

Fiberglass, plastic, or aluminum battens work well and do not require any finishing, but wood battens are still the best looking. Hardwoods like ash or mahogany or straight-grained softwoods like spruce and fir make fine battens. All wood battens should be well sealed with three coats of epoxy and a coat of varnish to retain their strength. Soaked wood will lose much of its stiffness and may snap in response to a gust of wind or sudden load.

Wood battens made for supporting a fabric structure usually need to be wider than they are thick to prevent twisting and to make rigging easier. We've had success with $\frac{1}{4}$-inch by $1\frac{1}{2}$-inch battens, but each application seems to require some experimentation as to best size and shape. Start big and keep shaving with a sharp block plane until the batten bends easily to the camber you want. This method also allows you to taper the end of a batten to provide a smaller radius or different shape, while leaving the center thicker and stiffer.

Laminated battens will be stiffer than solid battens and retain uniform strength. As discussed in Part II, you can laminate beams to almost any shape. First make the lofting board of $\frac{1}{2}$-inch-thick or $\frac{3}{4}$-inch-thick plywood; then draw the beams to full size right on the plywood. After you do all the layout, screw down short sections of aluminum angle and position the angles at the correct location for laminating by screwing the angles right to the board. We build battens with extreme curvature by using $\frac{1}{8}$-inch veneer, which will conform to complex shapes and will also retain the shape better than will thicker laminations. However, straight battens rolled up in the fabric allow a large structure to be stored easily in a small space.

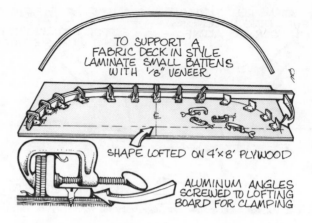

TO SUPPORT A FABRIC DECK IN STYLE LAMINATE SMALL BATTENS WITH 1/8" VENEER

SHAPE LOFTED ON 4'x8' PLYWOOD

ALUMINUM ANGLES SCREWED TO LOFTING BOARD FOR CLAMPING

Attachment Methods

Hold the outboard ends of decks, tents, and spray shields in place with snaps or loops and hooks. They can be attached to the gunwale, under the outwale, or, in the case of hooks, even inside the boat, if you drill a small hole under the gunwale to provide access. We favor shock cord loops and hooks as a means of attachment. They stretch in response to pressure or slack and will keep a fabric panel at about the same tautness whether wet, dry, hot, or cold. Using cords of various size and length also allows a degree of fine tuning. Be sure to buy the quality cord that comes in rolls. Diameters vary from ⅛ inch, which is good for small adjusting and lace lines, up to a whopping ½-inch diameter, which defies efforts to stretch it more than a few inches.

Don't stretch everything too tight, however. A bit of flex is often

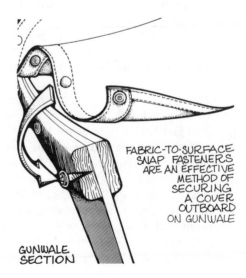

FABRIC-TO-SURFACE SNAP FASTENERS ARE AN EFFECTIVE METHOD OF SECURING A COVER OUTBOARD ON GUNWALE

GUNWALE SECTION

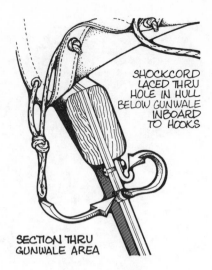

SHOCKCORD
LACED THRU
HOLE IN HULL
BELOW GUNWALE
INBOARD
TO HOOKS

SECTION THRU
GUNWALE AREA

desirable because a stiff and unyielding fabric structure will strain
lines, bend supports, and stretch or even tear fabric.

If hooks are permanently attached to the boat, any fabric structure can be set up easily even late at night or in wind and rain.

A couple of words of caution. Anchor your boat so it can weath-
ercock into the wind. If the wind blows into an open tent from the
backside, your ears will pop every time the thing flaps. Also, test
everything beforehand. Label battens of different lengths and check
for wear and tears. For some unknown reason, nothing ever seems
to happen to fabric decks or tents until late at night or in miserable
weather, when you least want to get up and deal with the situation.
We almost always rig everything and leave it for a few days on the
trailer to see if anything comes apart in wind or rain. If you're won-
dering how your tent will handle a 50-knot headwind, hook every-

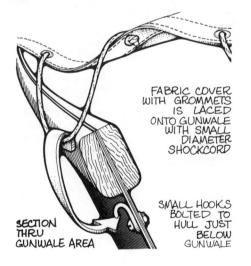

FABRIC COVER
WITH GROMMETS
IS LACED
ONTO GUNWALE
WITH SMALL
DIAMETER
SHOCKCORD

SMALL HOOKS
BOLTED TO
HULL JUST
BELOW
GUNWALE

SECTION
THRU
GUNWALE AREA

TENTS, DECKING, AND
SPRAY SHIELDS
173

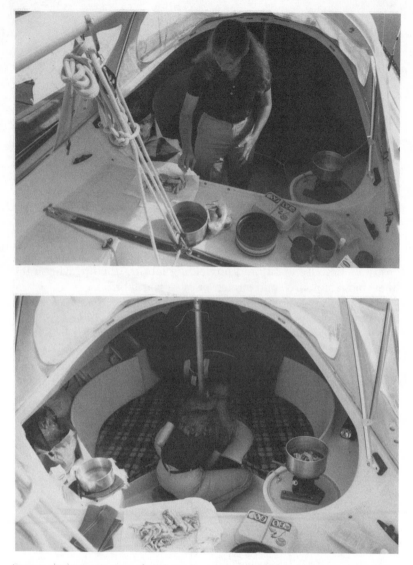

Canvas deck structures and an ingenious use of space transform a small daysailer into a successful cruiser. Above and facing page: With cockpit dodger in place there's standing headroom in the "galley," with a modular build-in to contain the stove (on top of a portable water tank), and a spacious countertop on the sheltered bridgedeck. When dinner is ready, the mast-mounted table slides up from its normal storage place on the sole, creating a saloon with comfortable sitting headroom. The cockpit boom tent provides additional privacy at the dock or anchorage. (Photos courtesy Alex Brown)

thing up and go for a drive. You may find that you need to rig additional lines fore and aft to provide proper support tension. It's a lot better to discover problems before you're in the midst of them.

Finally, be prepared in case something should fail. We always throw a few small C-clamps in the boat for overnight trips, since you can easily clamp a structure together in a pinch. Small plywood pads protect the hull and fabric from damage by the clamp heads. Sail tape or even duct tape will hold everything together until you can do a proper repair, so keep a roll handy.

Canvas Swing Seats

Simple canvas swing seats satisfy all requirements for small boat gear: They're lightweight, easy to build and stow, comfortable, and cheap. Unlike bulky, built-in furniture, they roll with the boat's motion, providing a much easier "ride," and they are movable or removable. By simply unsnapping them from the overhead support eyelets and snapping into another location, swing seats can be used from the forepeak to the stern and can be adjusted to work in the smallest of hulls.

Kids love to play in them. They will hold the cook in place in the galley so he has both hands free for cooking, and provide more seating space in the saloon when friends come aboard. A swing seat in the companionway also makes a cozy perch when keeping watch while the wind vane steers the boat. We even use our swing seat to hoist our 100-pound German Shepherd into and out of the dinghy.

We make our swing seats out of heavy polyester army duck, the same fabric we use for sail covers and dodgers. To make the basic seat, cut a 36-inch-square piece of cloth and fold it in half. Turn the edges under and stitch the envelope closed with a machine or by hand. If the fabric you choose feels weak, reinforce the sides with one-inch nylon webbing for extra support.

We beef up the corners with heavy leather scraps. (We bought a sackful for two dollars and had enough for dozens of projects.) Wide webbing is a suitable substitute. The extra thickness of leather or heavy webbing requires hand sewing with waxed nylon thread and and awl stitcher or a needle and sailor's palm. Don't forget to insert the stainless or bronze D-rings before you begin to sew.

Leave the support lines extra long so they can be adjusted as needed. If the seat pinches, place some extra support (like thin plywood) in the bottom of the seat, or just locate the overhead supports

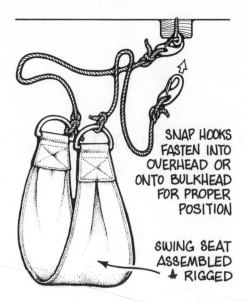

SNAP HOOKS
FASTEN INTO
OVERHEAD OR
ONTO BULKHEAD
FOR PROPER
POSITION

SWING SEAT
ASSEMBLED
& RIGGED

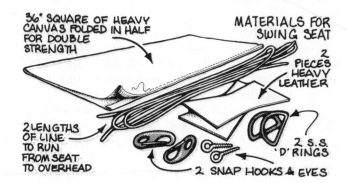

36" SQUARE OF HEAVY
CANVAS FOLDED IN HALF
FOR DOUBLE
STRENGTH

MATERIALS FOR
SWING SEAT

2
PIECES
HEAVY
LEATHER

2 LENGTHS
OF LINE
TO RUN
FROM SEAT
TO OVERHEAD

2 S.S.
'D' RINGS

2 SNAP HOOKS & EYES

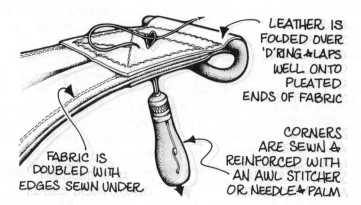

LEATHER IS
FOLDED OVER
'D' RING & LAPS
WELL ONTO
PLEATED
ENDS OF FABRIC

CORNERS
ARE SEWN &
REINFORCED WITH
AN AWL STITCHER
OR NEEDLE & PALM

FABRIC IS
DOUBLED WITH
EDGES SEWN UNDER

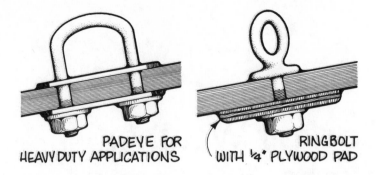

PADEYE FOR
HEAVY DUTY APPLICATIONS

RINGBOLT
WITH ¼" PLYWOOD PAD

farther apart. With some fiddling, it's also possible to make a swing seat with a fairly comfortable backrest by tying lines or shock cords across the back and adjusting them to proper length for comfort.

We tie a snap hook or carabiner in the ends of the support lines for quick release and attachment. The support eyes should be very small or placed in countersunk holes to save banging heads. Wooden cabin or deck beams make good strong mounting locations as do vertical bulkheads. Glass decks require through-bolting for proper support. Whatever it takes, be very sure that your mounting system is secure; if the swing were to pull out under duress, serious injury could result.

Cockpit Weather Cloths

Canvas weather cloths attached to the stanchions provide increased privacy (particularly in crowded moorages and packed marinas), give some protection from wind and spray, and generally make the cockpit safer and more comfortable. They are simple to make. Just sew a double ½-inch hem on all perimeter edges to reinforce the mounting grommets. Grommets planned in a pattern will allow easy lacing to the cockpit stanchions or cabin sides.

Some stanchions have small welded or bolted eyelets for dodger lace lines, or the mounting holes are simply drilled through the stanchion. All you need is a good mounting eyelet or hole at the top of each stanchion; the bottom can be held in place with eyelets attached to the deck. If the stanchions have a horizontal piece across the top, put lacing over the top for support. Each panel can be laced around the upright and into the next panel. All this takes some trial and error and adjusting to get just the right tension on the panels. We often use ⅛-inch diameter lace line, but shock cord has advantage because it allows a degree of elasticity and holds each panel taut under all conditions.

Really windproof weather cloths should be kept as tight as possible, but you should make provision for allowing water through should a solid wave slap them. It doesn't take much of a wave to bend small stanchions if they are tightly laced together. Leaving gaps on edges and bottoms of the canvas panels will be less windproof but safer in rough waters. If the water you're heading for has a bad reputation, you might even consider making the dodgers "breakaway" by using lighter cord for lashing, or by adding a Velcro slit in the middle that will tear open if hit by solid water.

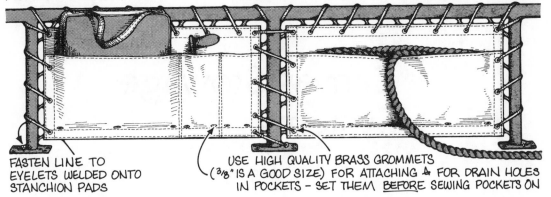

SELECT A HEAVY WATER·REPELLENT
ACRYLIC FABRIC WITH
MILDEW·RESISTANT FINISH

MEASURE AREA BETWEEN STANCHIONS & ADD
ABOUT 1½" TO ALL FOUR SIDES OR ENOUGH TO TURN
EDGES UNDER & FOLD OVER TO REINFORCE GROMMETS

FASTEN LINE TO
EYELETS WELDED ONTO
STANCHION PADS

USE HIGH QUALITY BRASS GROMMETS
(⅜" IS A GOOD SIZE) FOR ATTACHING & FOR DRAIN HOLES
IN POCKETS – SET THEM BEFORE SEWING POCKETS ON

When designing each panel, we try to sew canvas pockets to the inboard side for stowing lengths of line, winch handles, cushions, hand bearing compass, charts wrapped in plastic, and other things. Pockets can have shock cord sewn into their tops to make them tighter, or pleats to give them extra volume. The bottom corners of all sewn-in pockets should be vented with a grommet to drain any spray and rain water.

While most often used around the cockpit, weather cloths may also be appropriate along the sides of the foredeck. Although they increase windage, they make the foredeck more secure for kids and for sailbags. Larger panels that might otherwise obscure vision can be equipped with small sewn-in windows of clear acrylic.

Canvas Stowage Systems

Fabric stowage containers are particularly appropriate for small boat interiors because they are lightweight, easily modified to suit available space, and will often work in otherwise unused areas. A soft 10- to 20-ounce cotton duck is our choice for these compartments. It is available in a variety of colors that will match or complement any interior. These hanging compartments will also help to insulate and muffle bare, damp, and noisy fiberglass hulls.

Canvas stowage can be attached to just about any location inside the boat—overhead, inside lockers, in the bilge, and on the undersides of solid compartment hatches. Even usually unused spaces along the sheer clamp can be turned into valuable storage space.

We attach the compartments with Velcro snaps, screw caps and waxed wood screws, or lacing. Each of these methods permits easy removal for cleaning. Screws and screw caps work well in wood sheer clamps and ribs, but Velcro may be more appropriate inside a fiberglass hull.

Compartments fitted against the hull will provide a comfortable backrest, especially when stuffed full of clothes. We use shock cord or strips of Velcro to hold items in place. Canvas compartments can also make quiet, individual storage spots for noisy pots and pans that won't fit anywhere else without making a racket.

Before cutting, wash the new fabric in hot water and dry it in a hot dryer to eliminate subsequent shrinkage. Also remember to add extra inches for the folds required for finishing the edges on all sides.

Fabric compartments made of quality materials, good weatherproof fabric, and stainless steel fastenings or Velcro, are also good for use in small open boats or in open cockpits. For years, we used

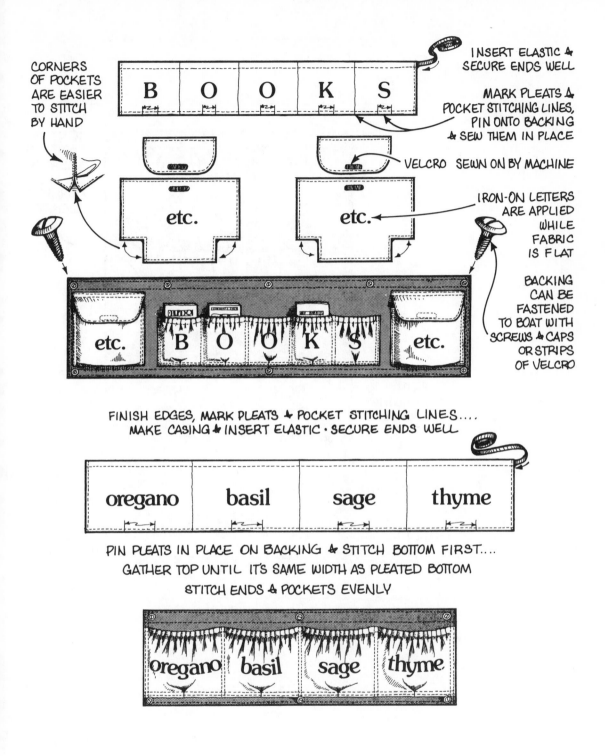

CORNERS OF POCKETS ARE EASIER TO STITCH BY HAND

INSERT ELASTIC & SECURE ENDS WELL

MARK PLEATS & POCKET STITCHING LINES, PIN ONTO BACKING & SEW THEM IN PLACE

B O O K S

etc.

etc.

VELCRO SEWN ON BY MACHINE

IRON-ON LETTERS ARE APPLIED WHILE FABRIC IS FLAT

BACKING CAN BE FASTENED TO BOAT WITH SCREWS & CAPS OR STRIPS OF VELCRO

etc.   **B O O K S**   etc.

FINISH EDGES, MARK PLEATS & POCKET STITCHING LINES....
MAKE CASING & INSERT ELASTIC · SECURE ENDS WELL

oregano   basil   sage   thyme

PIN PLEATS IN PLACE ON BACKING & STITCH BOTTOM FIRST....
GATHER TOP UNTIL IT'S SAME WIDTH AS PLEATED BOTTOM
STITCH ENDS & POCKETS EVENLY

oregano   basil   sage   thyme

CANVAS STOWAGE
SYSTEMS
183

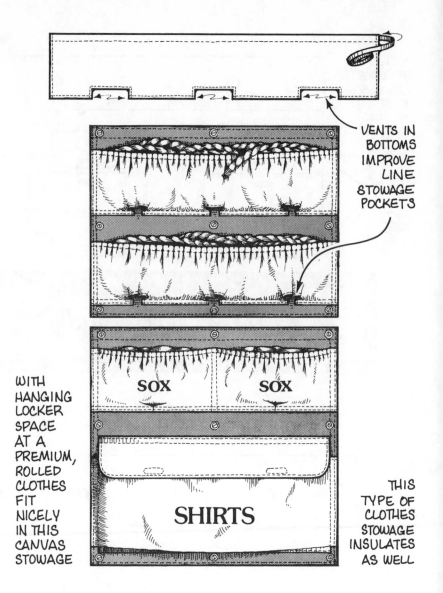

VENTS IN
BOTTOMS
IMPROVE
LINE
STOWAGE
POCKETS

WITH
HANGING
LOCKER
SPACE
AT A
PREMIUM,
ROLLED
CLOTHES
FIT
NICELY
IN THIS
CANVAS
STOWAGE

SOX   SOX

SHIRTS

THIS
TYPE OF
CLOTHES
STOWAGE
INSULATES
AS WELL

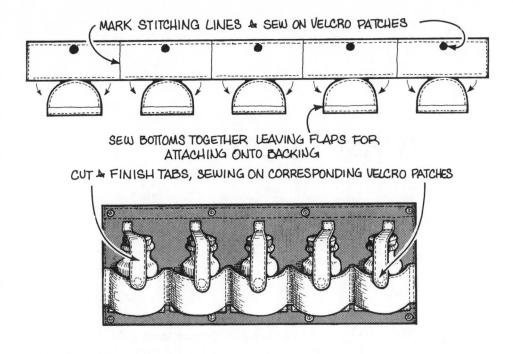

MARK STITCHING LINES & SEW ON VELCRO PATCHES

SEW BOTTOMS TOGETHER LEAVING FLAPS FOR
ATTACHING ONTO BACKING

CUT & FINISH TABS, SEWING ON CORRESPONDING VELCRO PATCHES

a multi-pocketed compartment to hold gear and lunch bags in a small, sliding-seat rowing dory, and the compartment was easily removed for stowing in the larger boat. Attached to the transom, it kept everything out of any water in the bottom of the hull and was easily accessible.

Mast Boots

Whether a keel-stepped mast goes through the cabin top or through the deck, it still has to be provided with a waterproof boot to prevent leakage through the mast opening. The ideal boot should look ship-shape and be removable without a great deal of effort.

Though the boot shown in the accompanying illustration is for an unstayed mast, the arrangement is almost the same for a stayed rig. The fabric for the boot can be a scrap of heavy marine canvas. Instead of more traditional methods, we use a stainless steel hose clamp to encircle the mast. Make sure the clamp is really stainless steel and doesn't have parts that will rust and bleed on the fabric. The boot is laid out in an open cone shape, and the edges are sewn together in position around the mast. Fold the fabric in a flat felled position (see top illustration) and sew a straight stitch by hand. Turn the boot up with the inside out and stuff the top edge down into the loose hose clamp and tighten. Pull the boot down over the clamp and position it on the deck around the mast. Don't pull down so tightly that the clamp cuts into the fabric.

To further waterproof the boat, you might want to attach the canvas to a circular plywood molding glued and screwed to the deck, but normally it is perfectly adequate to attach it right to the deck. For wood decks, bronze tacks or anchorfast nails work well. Fiberglass decks will probably require stainless steel self-tapping screws and stainless steel washers to prevent bleeding. Bronze is an even better choice and also looks very nautical.

Double the fabric under the hem, leaving enough to nail or screw flat to the deck, and place fastenings around the perimeter, spaced approximately one inch apart.

After the boot is in place, we saturate the fabric with unboiled

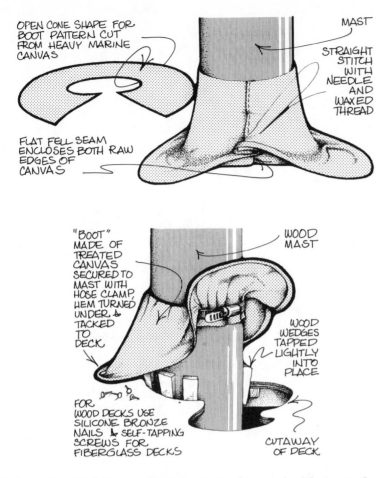

OPEN CONE SHAPE FOR BOOT PATTERN CUT FROM HEAVY MARINE CANVAS

MAST

STRAIGHT STITCH WITH NEEDLE AND WAXED THREAD

FLAT FELL SEAM ENCLOSES BOTH RAW EDGES OF CANVAS

"BOOT" MADE OF TREATED CANVAS SECURED TO MAST WITH HOSE CLAMP, HEM TURNED UNDER & TACKED TO DECK

WOOD MAST

WOOD WEDGES TAPPED LIGHTLY INTO PLACE

FOR WOOD DECKS USE SILICONE BRONZE NAILS & SELF-TAPPING SCREWS FOR FIBERGLASS DECKS

CUTAWAY OF DECK

linseed oil, which leaves a thick protective film on the fabric's surface. We make two applications, let it dry for a few days, then apply a small bead of silicone around the top edge against the mast and on the deck against the boot. The boot should be flexible, and if you've used good fabric, it will last a long time.

Part VII
Off-Season

Cradles

When the leaves turn yellow and the delightful aroma of wood smoke swirls around the boatyard, it is time to think of laying up for the winter. One convenient thing about small boats is how easy they are to lift and move about, even by an amateur with limited equipment and expertise. In fact, many small boats can be hauled and stored right on the trailer. But if your boat gravitates toward the heftier end of the "small boat" category, there will come a time when you find yourself needing to build or rebuild a cradle.

A cradle has three basic structural components. At the bottom are the fore-and-aft side beams, which form the base of the cradle and sometimes also function as its runners. Across these fore-and-aft beams lie the crosspiece beams, which bear the weight of the hull. Stability is provided by uprights, or "shores"—vertical timbers with diagonal bracing, attached stoutly to the cradle frame at various locations. Some hulls can get by with one pair of shores port and starboard and good bracing at the bow and transom, but most cradles have two pairs of shores to distribute strain and provide a well-tailored fit, necessary for proper support.

Design

The crosspiece beams bear the weight of the hull. Normally they should be the same dimensional size as the fore-and-aft beams, but if the cradle is for a large boat, eight feet or more in beam, they may need to be heftier to support the weight of the boat over the wider span. Boats weighing less than a ton usually can be supported by 2 x 4s—either a number of individual pieces placed on edge, or three or four pairs bolted together and placed on edge. Boats up to 6,000

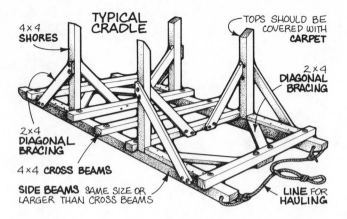

TYPICAL CRADLE

4×4 SHORES

TOPS SHOULD BE COVERED WITH CARPET

2×4 DIAGONAL BRACING

2×4 DIAGONAL BRACING

4×4 CROSS BEAMS

SIDE BEAMS SAME SIZE OR LARGER THAN CROSS BEAMS

LINE FOR HAULING

pounds need larger dimensional lumber: either 4 x 4s, or 2 x 4s (or 2 x 6s) bolted together. (There are, in fact, decided advantages to the latter method: the 2 x 4s are less expensive and less prone to splitting than the larger beams, particularly when laminated together.) Six crosspiece beams are recommended to support weights in excess of one ton.

The shores, or upright supports, extend vertically from the cradle base, usually supported by the fore-and-aft beams, to provide side support to the hull. The tops of the shores should be fitted to the contour of the hull and covered with a scrap of carpeting to avoid abrasion. Cradles built for use with only one boat can be fitted exactly to the hull shape by cutting each shore slightly short and attaching an extension at just the right angle to the hull. A cradle can also be designed to accommodate hulls of various sizes and shapes by making the shores adjustable up and down and in and out.

Most cradles will be very difficult to keep square without diagonals positioned at critical places throughout the structure. Under the crosspiece beams is one such place. Each of the uprights usually also needs one or two diagonals for alignment and support.

Materials

If possible, buy rough sawn wood for cradles: it's less expensive and often slightly larger dimension and stronger than finished beams. Fir is a good choice for cradles since it's strong and available in most lumberyards. Pressure-treated wood is an option, but unless you are building an adjustable cradle for long-term or commercial use, the additional expense is probably not worth it. Most cradles are simply oiled or painted and last for years without problems.

Cradles work a lot when they are moved around, putting considerable strain on the fastenings. Spikes or large nails can be used for assembly, but bolts provide a much more secure yet flexible fastening, particularly for large structural members. The other advantage of bolts, if you're building the cradle out of green lumber, is that they

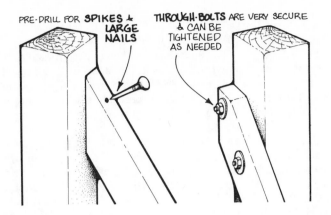

permit retightening of the fastenings as the wood shrinks. Carriage bolts work well in small cradles, but for larger ones built of 4 x 4s, you may be better off with regular bolts, to which you can apply a wrench at either end. When bolting through the bottom of the fore-and-aft pieces, be sure to countersink the bolt heads well so that the runners will slide easily, or use round "carriage" heads on the bottom.

Spikes and large nails are used mostly for temporary bracing and to hold blocking and wedges in place. When using spikes in small dimension timbers it may be worthwhile to predrill to ensure that the spike doesn't split and weaken the timber.

Moving and Blocking

It is common to drag or roll cradles to and from the water using a vehicle or a come-along winch, and you should locate attachment points for a tow cable on both ends of the cradle. Sometimes the easiest method is to drill large-diameter holes through the ends of the fore-and-aft beams through which you can run a chain or a line. The bottom of the cradle should be tapered to slide easily over obstructions.

Cradles are often dragged around using the fore-and-aft pieces as runners, but another method—far easier on the cradle—is to move it using long rollers under the base. It is important that the rollers be long; short sections are difficult to keep aligned and usually only work for a short time before they roll out from under the cradle and need to be replaced. With long rollers even a large, heavy hull can be moved, slowly and in small, safe increments. The hull can also be maneuvered sideways by aligning all the rollers in the desired direction. Lumberyards sometimes sell perfectly round logs, called peelers, which are the cores left after veneer has been removed. These work very well for rolling hulls.

Some owners launch their boats simply by pushing the cradle-with-hull down to the intertidal zone at low tide and waiting for the tide to rise, lifting the hull out of the cradle (or into it for the haulout

Temporary Frames

Many hull supports are built for temporary use only, to hold hulls while owners work on them or trim them out. Sometimes they are little more than braces against the hull sides while the keel sits on blocks on the ground.

A-frames are handy for working around small boats and may even temporarily take the place of a cradle. An A-frame is made from 2 x 4s or 2 x 6s bolted together near the top end to form a freestanding, self-supporting ladder. Eight-foot studs are normally adequate for the uprights, and three or four 2 x 4s in stud length or somewhat shorter lengths are nailed or bolted across to serve as scaffolding platforms and/or ladder rungs. Diagonals for additional support are attached to the back side of the frame.

The frames can be adjusted for stability by moving the legs farther apart or closer together. A line should be tied from one leg to the other to act as a stop, preventing the A-frame from sliding all the way open and collapsing on a slick surface.

A-frames can be used for temporary bracing as well. One pair of frames positioned port and starboard near the bow and another near the stern will provide adequate side support for a small boat when nailed or clamped together with 1 x 4 bracing. (The weight of the boat, as usual, should be supported from beneath.) This arrangement can also be used to move a hull around in a yard or out of the shop into the yard.

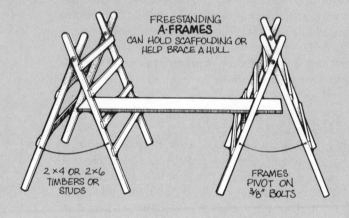

FREESTANDING **A·FRAMES** CAN HOLD SCAFFOLDING OR HELP BRACE A HULL

2 x 4 OR 2 x 6 TIMBERS OR STUDS

FRAMES PIVOT ON 3⁄8" BOLTS

operation). This strategy usually works quite well as long as the cradle stays on the bottom, but if it lifts along with the boat, it may damage the boat, or you may not be able to separate the two. Consider ballasting the cradle to keep it on the bottom until the hull has floated clear.

Once your boat is in its cradle for the season, you need to make sure that it is sitting level, so that self-draining lockers and cockpits will function normally all winter. If the bottom of the keel is parallel with the waterline, then leveling the cradle will also level the hull. If the keel is not parallel with the waterline, it may be necessary to shim with blocks on the crosspiece beams to get the hull level. The alternative method is to jack up one end of the cradle and block under the cradle base.

Covers

A good cover can reduce seasonal preparation to an easy weekend of touching up varnish and cleaning—as opposed to days of radical scraping, sanding, varnishing, and repainting.

Frames

The success of a cover usually rests on the framework beneath. A frame provides a well-sloped support system for the cover, preventing droops and sags and encouraging rain to run off rather than collect in the middle. A well-designed frame also holds the cover off the boat, permitting air circulation below. This is vital to wood hulls and a benefit to boats of all types. A snug-fitting, waterproof cover makes it possible to leave hatches partially open all winter, greatly reducing mold and mildew.

On a small sailboat stored with its mast in place, the simplest frame is simply to use the boom as a ridgepole. The cover can be designed with a slit to fit around the mast, and the angle is usually a good one to encourage rain run-off. If the mast is to be taken out, it can sometimes be positioned on top of the boat and used as a ridgepole. Be sure the cover is wide enough to run outboard of the caprails, so that water will drain away from the hull.

On a powerboat or a sailboat whose mast will be stored elsewhere, it is necessary to construct a freestanding frame. Wood is probably the most common choice of material. A custom framework can be made of 1 x 4s (or 1 x 6s for longer spans), placed on three-foot centers, or even four-foot centers for larger boats. Small boats can use smaller-dimension wood placed on closer centers—16 to 18 inches. Fastening with small screws, rather than nails, makes the

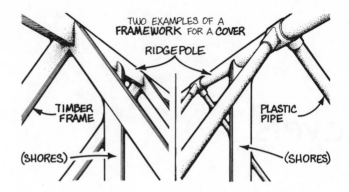

TWO EXAMPLES OF A
FRAMEWORK FOR A **COVER**

RIDGEPOLE

TIMBER
FRAME

PLASTIC
PIPE

(SHORES)

(SHORES)

frames easy to disassemble and reassemble. Simply mark the pieces forward to aft, port and starboard, and replace them in the same sequence each storage season.

Frames can also be constructed of metal pipe or PVC plastic pipe. The latter, with all its available elbows and connections, is a particularly good choice. It's lighter than metal, easier to work with, and not as prone to rusting. It's also flexible enough to permit a departure from traditional ridgepole design, allowing the construction of interesting and efficient shapes. PVC pipe is readily available at building and plumbing supply houses. Diameters as small as ½ inch are adequate for small boats; ¾-inch and 1-inch diameters are appropriate for larger boats.

Attaching the framework to the boat is always a challenge, usually best solved by individual ingenuity. The outboard legs can sometimes be attached to stanchions (or even slipped over them if you're working with PVC pipe). Other tiedown options include hawseholes and deck hardware. Some owners have even resorted to adding vertical extensions to their cradles to provide anchoring points for the frames. However you solve the problem, make sure that the attachment system is strong, so that frame and cover don't collapse or blow away in the first winter storm.

Frames can be individual units, but sometimes thin furring strips are added, running fore and aft, to tie the structure together, providing

HEAVY **FABRIC** OR **LEATHER**
TIED TO ENDS OF FRAMEWORK
TO **PREVENT CHAFING** DECK

stable spacing and an additional measure of stiffness. As with the frames themselves, furring strips are best attached with small screws rather than nails to make the structure easy to disassemble and reassemble. They can also be attached using small plastic ties or small-diameter shock cord, which provides a degree of elasticity.

The frames must be well rounded to protect the cover, and it never hurts to pad all corners with carpet remnants held in place with duct tape or plastic ties.

Covers

Covers should be strong enough to support an occasional load of snow and to cope with gusts of wind from any direction. There is a variety of fabric options available, ranging from cheap 6- to 9-mil plastic that lasts one season at most to sturdy canvas and cotton duck. You don't usually save any money in the long run buying cheap fabric.

Among the most popular solutions nowadays are those garish blue or orange "reinforced" plastic tarps. They are all cheap imports, made of inferior materials that will rip without warning after some exposure and are difficult to patch, even with duct tape. By about the beginning of the third season they tend to start cracking and flaking away, leaving small pieces of colored plastic all over the boat, and as they flog and chafe they are highly abrasive to varnish or gelcoat. They are popular only because they are the cheapest "quick-fix" solution.

Sturdy, heavier-mil plastic is a useful option in some situations. Plastic does not protect the boat from sunlight, but does admit useful light for working on the boat while covered. White or off-white plastic will stay noticeably cooler, but there is nothing wrong with darker colors in higher latitudes where the extra heat may be beneficial. One concern with colors is that they occasionally stain the deck and topsides. Clear plastic, of course, eliminates this problem and provides the maximum working light, if that is your objective.

Old-fashioned, cotton canvas tarps make good boat covers and will last for many seasons if properly maintained. They are available in a variety of weights, and some come with paraffin or chemical waterproofing and mildew treatments. Weights of 10 to 18 ounces per square yard are appropriate for boat covers. Even if you need a custom-tailored cover, the most economical option may be to buy a rectangular cotton canvas tarp and cut it to size.

Cotton duck has long been popular among outfitters and tent makers, for reasons that also make it a good choice for boat covers. The fabric's open weave provides excellent ventilation, and when wet the weave swells shut, making the fabric watertight. The negative aspect of this quality is that cotton duck also stays wet longer than canvas and may rot or mildew more easily.

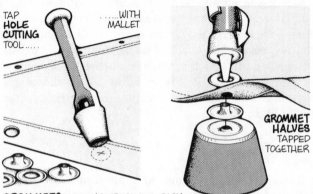

TAP **HOLE CUTTING** TOOL ....WITH MALLET

GROMMET **HALVES** TAPPED TOGETHER

GROMMETS ARE INEXPENSIVE & EASY TO ADD TO JUST ABOUT ANY COVER OR TARP WITH THE **BASIC TOOLS**

Regardless of the material, covers need good hems and grommets around the perimeter, and there should be an adequate number of tiedown points to ensure that the cover is secured tightly. Loose-fitting covers that flap excessively will wear out faster than well-supported, well-fitted covers tied securely in place. Tight-fitting covers for small boats may need a tiedown point every 18 to 24 inches; for larger boats, a tiedown every four feet is normally adequate. A grommet kit will allow you to install tiedown points as needed.

Where there are insufficient attachment points on the boat or cradle, small sandbags may provide sufficient holding power to keep a well-fitted cover in place, even in a high wind. Properly sewn webbing loops (see illustration) provide added convenience in arranging an efficient tiedown system. They can be as long or as short as needed to loop over a piece of hardware on a boat. Lengths of shock cord can be used in place of webbing loops, or simply looped through a

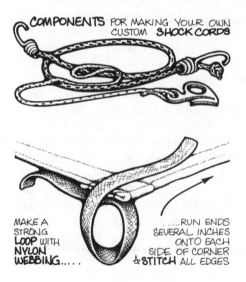

COMPONENTS FOR MAKING YOUR OWN CUSTOM **SHOCK CORDS**

MAKE A STRONG **LOOP** WITH **NYLON WEBBING**..... .....RUN ENDS SEVERAL INCHES ONTO EACH SIDE OF CORNER & **STITCH** ALL EDGES

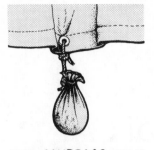

SMALL **SANDBAGS** TIED TO
GROMMETS IN HEM CAN
HELP TO **HOLD COVER** IN PLACE

grommet hole, to allow you to adjust to a constant tension. A shock
cord-rigged cover, once built and tuned, can be very quickly installed
and removed. An additional advantage to such a system is that it
automatically adjusts to the swelling and shrinking of the cover when
hot, cold, wet, or dry.

Good canvas or cotton duck covers will last 15 years or more if
well designed and maintained, and properly stored when not in use.
Proper storage means drying the cover completely—washing it first
if it has collected an unusual amount of dirt or salt—and making sure
there is enough ventilation in the storage area to prevent mildew and
mold.

Appendix A
Directory of Suppliers

The following directory is by no means intended to be inclusive; it is simply a list of suppliers—most of them already mentioned in the text—whom we have found helpful in various aspects of building and upgrading small boats. Other sources are readily available by consulting boating magazines. For a comprehensive directory of specialty lumber suppliers, see *Boatbuilding Woods: A Directory of Suppliers* (WoodenBoat, 1988, distributed by International Marine Publishing Company).

GOUGEON BROTHERS/WEST EPOXY. PO Box 908, Bay City, MI 48707. (517) 684–7286.

> For epoxy, fiberglass cloth, tape, graphite fibers, fillers, instructional literature, safety gear, and accessories.

DEAN COMPANY. Box 426, Gresham, OR 97030. (503) 665–2161.

> For quality slice cut (not rotary peeled) veneer of various species, both hard and soft woods. Teak, douglas fir, spruce, western red cedar, etc. They also ship small amounts.

SIMPSON TIMBER CO. Third and Franklin, Shelton, WA 98584. (206) 426–6202.

> For hardwood plywood of various species and types for boatbuilding.

BECKSON MARINE INC. 165 Holland Avenue, Box 3336, Bridgeport, CT 06605. (203) 333–1412.

> For plastic ports, pumps, vents, window tracks, and related accessories.

PUGET SOUND TENT AND AWNING. 620 S. Industrial Way, Seattle, WA 98108. (206) 622-8219.

> For canvas, vinyl, and other fabrics.

SEATTLE FABRICS. 3876 Bridge Way N., Seattle, WA 98103. (206) 632-6022.

For canvas and other boat fabric.

CANE AND BASKET SUPPLY CO. 1283 S. Cochran, Los Angeles, CA 90019. (213) 939–9644.

Index

Blocks, backing (butt), 35–38; installation, 40–41; locking mechanisms, 118

Boiler punchings, 20, 89

Bolts, 17; for building cradles, 192–93; drilling and insertion, 39–40; for hull-to-deck connection, 44; installing beams, 55; removal, 38; rudder, 74; samson post, 68. *See also* Locking mechanisms

Bow eyes, 38

Bow rollers, 71–72

Braces: hardwood for ports, 96; in veneer hull liners, 124–25

Bulkheads: construction, 60–63; finishing, 64–65; fittings in, 63–64; partial, as mast support, 58; partial, patterning for, 17; partial, to solve oil canning, 45; patterning, 60–63; patterning stick, 60–61; shortcomings, 35; ultralight, 59; use with samson post, 68; watertight, 86; weak, 59; with hull liners, 60

Bunk bottoms: nettings, 155; patterning, 17. *See also* Pipe berths

C

Cabinetry: face frames, 143–44; modular, 17, 142–47; patterning and framings, 142–44

Cabin sole, patterning, 17

Canvas, 159–87; sources for, 159; suitability for small boats, 159–61; winter boat covers, 197–99

Carbon fiber, 75–76

Cardboard, use for patterning, 60

Carriage bolts, 55. *See also* Bolts

Caulkings, 17, 43, 56

Ceilings, 121–24; beam and panel, 123–24

Cellophane, for lamps, 149

Centerboards, repair and reinforcement of, 73–77

Chainplates, 5, 37–42; fastenings, 17; mounting, 40–41; problems, 37–42; strap-type, 38

Chart table, portable, 149

Cheeks. *See* Doublers

Chocks, 37–38

Chopper gun, 19, 36

Cleats: access to, 38; fastenings for, 17; support cleats, 69, 70, 108, 132

CO_2 canisters, 90

Coamings, beddings for, 108; for hatch units, 104, 105–8, 109

Colloidal silica. *See* Epoxy, thickened

Compartments, fabric, for open boats, 182–83; for flotation, 85–86; for hull strength, 85–86; interior, location of, 131; self-draining, 115–18; watertight, in bilge, 86. *See also* Lockers

Compression pads, 42

Corrosion, in fiberglass laminate, 38, 39

Countertops, 141–47

Covers: canvas companionway, 162; fabric decking and tents, 168–

76; insulated, 162–63; support systems for, 168–71, 195, 196; winter, 195–99. *See also* Canvas

Cradles, 191–94

Cutouts, 9–10, 12, 14, 36, 51, 54, 96, 127–28. *See also* Template

D

Deadlights. *See under* Portlights

Deck beams. *See* Beams, exterior

Deck overlays, wood, 55–56

Deck plates, 87

Decking, fabric, 168–76

Decks: camber of, 107; fiberglass, 56; plywood, 50; reinforcements for, 50–72; teak, 56

Doors, 144–47; fabric facings for, 145; flush fitted, 146; hanging procedure, 146–47; hollow core, 145; offset hinges for, 146; panels for, 145; submarine type, 86

Doublers: for bulkheads, 59; for plywood decks, 69; for rudders, 76

Drain holes: in lockers, 115–17; in weathercloth pockets, 181

Drawers, 144–45

Drills and bits, 7–10

Duck, cotton stowage compartments, 182

Duck, cotton: for boat covers, 197; for stowage compartments, 182; storage of, 199

Duck, polyester: for swing seats, 177

Dust, fiberglass, 10, 11, 15

Dutchman, use in rudder repair, 74

E

Ear protection, 11, 15

Edge guides, 12–14

Epoxy, 5–6, 25–26; as bedding material, 42, 69–70; bolt hole repairs, 39, 58; bulkhead chambers, sealing, 59; cored laminate, sealing, 45; compatibility with foam, 75; deck beams, laminating, 53, 55, 57; degradation from ultraviolet, 47, 116; graphite powder, mixing, 71; as moisture barrier, 47; plywood sealing, 40, 41, 42, 57, 58, 69, 91, 98, 108, 111–12, 125, 128, 132; rudder repair, 74–75; safety, 6; sanding, 6; sinks, 139–41; water tanks, 135–38; WEST system, 6, 42. *See also* Fillets

Epoxy, thickened: as bedding, 42, 69–70; as caulking, 69–70; coaming joints, sealing, 106; colloidal silica, 31, 40, 76, 77, 124–25; for fairing and smoothing, 27, 49; for fillets, 30–31, 108; for filling bolt holes, 40; for gluing, 65, 67, 124–25; microballoons, 27, 31, 75, 76, 125; premixed fillers, 31; rudder repair, 75–77; surfaces, smoothing, 27; with veneer, 65, 124–25; wood and hardware fastenings, sealing, 66, 72, 106

F

Fabrics. *See* Canvas

Face frames, 143–44

Fastenings. *See* Bolts, Fillets, Screws

Fastening, 17; correcting problems, 37, 38–42. *See also* Epoxy; Epoxy, thickened

Fiberglass: components of, 20–26; curing time, 26; cutting and drilling, 7–16; finishing, 14–16; "itch factor," 30; overlapping, 28, 30, 39; sanding, 14–16, 30; saturation of, 28–30; sheathing over wood, 23; tape, 24–25, 49; tools, 26–27; types, 21–25. *See also* Laminate

Fillers. *See* Epoxy, thickened

Fillets, epoxy, 30–32; for bulkheads, 36, 62, 64; compartments, 90, 116; deck beams, 55; glass tape (use with), 25; gusset reinforcement, 48, 142; hatches, 106, 108; ports, 102; ribs, 46; rudder repair, 77; samson post, 68–69; storage tanks, 136–37

Flange, perimeter, 43, 44

Floor timbers, strengthening, 47–48

Flotation, 79–90; arrangement of, 82; backup systems, 90; factory-installed, 87; negative, 81; positive, by bulkheads, 59; overall requirements, 81–82

Foam: Airex, 123; closed cell, 83; compatibility with resin, 75; for flotation, 83–85; Klegecell, 123; packing "peanuts", 84–85; ping-pong balls, 83

Formica, 147

Frames: temporary, for hull support, 194; for decking and tents, 168–71; for modular cabinetry, 142–44; for winter covers, 195–97

Furring strips, 196–97

Futons, 166–67

G

Gelcoat, 20; marking and scoring, 7, 9; sanding, 14; protective sealing, 47; wax removal, 49

Goggles, 11

Grabrails, as deck reinforcements, 50

Grates, plywood, 126–29

Grommets: kits, 164; use with weather cloths, 180–81

Gussets, plywood: for strengthening hull, 48; support for samson posts, 68

H

Hardboard (Masonite), 149

Hardware, flush fitting, for hatches, 117

Hardware problems, 37–42

Hatchboards, 110, 111–14

Hatchcovers: butterfly, 117; clearance for, 106–07; flush-fitting, 131–33; see-through, 107; sliding, 110, 114–15; watertight, 87

Hatches, 5, 104–15; assembly, 105–08; centerline support, 117; companionway, 110–14; complete units, 104–9; installation, 11, 108–9; location, 105; locking mechanisms, 109–10, 114; squaring, 106

Hatchtops. *See* Hatchcovers

Hawsepipe, to lead anchor chain, 117

Hinges, 109, 117, 146; piano, 103, 151

Hull liners. *See* Liners

Hull reinforcements, 43–49, 86

Hull-to-deck connection, 43–44

I

Inspection plates, 36, 48

Insulation, 59, 123; insulated covers, 162–63

J

Jigs. *See under* Templates

Jigsaw. *See under* Saws

K

Keel bolts, use with samson posts, 66

Klegecell, 123

Knees: to strengthen bulkheads, 59; for tables, 151

L

Lace line, use with weather cloths, 180

Laminate: building up of, 45; repairing, 39–40; water absorption by, 47. *See also* Fiberglass

Laminating forms, 53

Laminates, plastic, 147

Lead, as ballast, 89

Leaks, in hull-to-deck connection, 43–44

Leather, 177

Lexan: door panels, 145; hatchcovers, 107; ports, 99

Lifelines, netting for, 155

Light, ultraviolet, 20, 47, 116

Liners, hull, 36, 124–25; considerations in adding bulkheads, 60; cutting into, 39; veneer, 124–25

Linseed oil, on mast boots, 186–87

Lockers: anchor, 116–17; designing, 130–31; interior, 130–34; securing, 118; self-draining, 115–18, 194

Locking mechanisms, 109–10, 114, 118, 133

M

Mast boots, 186–87
Mast, support for, 4, 5, 37, 50, 56–59
Microballoons. *See* Epoxy, thickened
Moisture barrier, 47
Moldings: on bulkhead edges, 64; plywood, 186; rubber channel, 100; teak, 112; transom reinforcement, 49

N

Nails, 193
Netting, 155–56

O

Oil canning, 44, 50

P

Paint, non-skid, 128
Paneling, tongue-and-groove, 59
Patterning, 17–18, 48, 60–62
Patterning stick, 60–62
Piano hinges. *See under* Hinges
Pilot hole, 17
Pin, for samson post, 60
Pintles and gudgeons, 74
Pipe berths, 164–65
Plexiglas: door panels, 145; hatchcovers, 107; ports, 99
Plywood: backing blocks, 40–41, 44; beams, 51, 52–55; bilge compartments, 86; bow rollers, 71–72; bulkheads, 59–65; cabinetry, 142–47; ceilings, 123–24; chart table, 149; coamings, 105; compression pads, 42; decks, 50; decreasing port size, 98–99; doublers, 59, 69, 76; grates, 126–29; hatchboards, 111–12; hatches, 104–7; lockers, 116; mast support pad, 57–58; molding, 186; patterning with, 18, 61; pump board, 91; rudder repair, 75–76; sinks, 139–41; splines, 62; storm shutters, 96; tanks, 135–38; templates, 12–13
Portlights, 95–103; flush-fitting, 98; in hatchboards, 113; hinged, 103; homemade, 99–102; installation, 97–99; positioning, 96–97; reducing size of, 98–99; sealed (deadlights), 96; sliding, 102–3
Ports. *See under* Portlights
Privacy, 99, 180
Pumps and pump boards, 91

Q

Quarter-sawn wood, 105–6

R

S

Stiffeners, hull, 45–47, 87. *See also* Reinforcements
Stop collar, 17
Stowage systems: build-ins, 130–34, 142–47; canvas, 182–85; netting, 155–56; storage tanks, 135–38. *See also* Lockers
Stress fractures, 37
Stress points, 38
Strongback, 58
Support cleats. *See under* Cleats
Support pad, mast, 57–58
Support systems, for tents and covers. *See under* Frames
Surface preparation for fiberglassing, 27–28
Surform tool, 75
Swings, canvas, 177–79

T

Tables, 148–54; chart table, 149
Tanks, water and storage, 135–138; plumbing systems for, 138, 140; portable, 136, 140; sinks, 139–41
Templates, 7, 11, 12–14; jigs, 127. *See also* Patterning stick
Tents, cockpit and deck, 168–76
Timbers: floor, 5, 47–48; solid, for deck beams, 53. *See also* Beams, exterior
Through-hull fixtures, 10, 12, 13, 90
Toerails, as deck reinforcements, 50
Toggles, 133
Tools: fiberglassing, 26–27; hand, 16; power 7–15
Towing bitts. *See* Samson posts
Transducers. *See* Through-hull fixtures
Transom reinforcements, 49

V

Velcro, 151, 162
Ventilation, 111, 145, 197; working with epoxy, 6, 26
Veneer: for bulkhead finishing, 64–65; deck overlays, 56; hull liners, 124–25; mast support pad, 57; strengthening ports, 99
Vinyl covers, 162

W

Water absorption, by laminate, 38, 39, 42, 45, 47, 73
Water storage systems. *See under* Tanks
Waterline, 81
Watersoak damage. *See under* Water absorption
Watertight divisions: bulkheads, 59; compartments, 86. *See also* Flotation
Weather cloths, 180–82